GIVING THE BODY A LIFT BY USING YOUR SPIRITUAL GIFTS

RANDY PETERSEN
▼●◆■
DON COUSINS

Cook Ministry Resources
a division of Cook Communications Ministries
Colorado Springs, Colorado/Paris, Ontario

Giving the Body a Lift by Using Your Spiritual Gifts
Christian LifeStyle Series

© 1993 David C. Cook Publishing Co.

Cook Ministry Resources
a division of Cook Communications Ministries
4050 Lee Vance View; Colorado Springs, CO 80918-7100
Cable address: DCCOOK
Designed by Randy Maid
Cover illustration by Guy Wolek
Inside illustrations by Bruce Van Patter
Printed in U.S.A.

ISBN: 0-7814-5026-8

C ▾ O • N ◆ T ■ E ▾ N • T ◆ S

Introduction: **Are You Ready for a Christian Lifestyle?**   4

Leader's Overview by Don Cousins   6

Seven Sessions by Randy Petersen

Session 1: **Who Am I?**
Identifying Ourselves As Gifted Children of God   11

Session 2: **Where Do I Fit In?**
Finding Our Place in God's Community   21

Session 3: **What Can I Say?**
Unwrapping the Speaking Gifts   31

Session 4: **What Can I Do?**
Opening Up the Serving Gifts   47

Session 5: **Do I Have a Sign Gift?**
Unraveling the Sign Gifts   61

Session 6: **What Did I Get?**
Discovering Our Specific Spiritual Gifts   73

Session 7: **How Can I Use It?**
Learning to Use Our Spiritual Gifts   85

ARE YOU READY FOR A CHRISTIAN LIFESTYLE?

Ever noticed that you can swim along for years in the Christian life without leaving the shallow end of the pool? Then one day it hits you: If you're going to *do* anything about your faith, you've got to go deeper. If you're going to have a truly satisfying walk with God, you've got to plunge past surface spirituality, empty words, faith without action.

But you're wary. What will a really *Christian* lifestyle be like? Will you have to over-commit yourself? Will God demand the impossible of you? Will you have to erase your personality and become a musty, dusty saint from the pre-TV, pre-stereo, pre-microwave days?

Commitment for Today's Adults

Wary—that's how many of today's adults feel when they're urged to be "on fire for the Lord." They want to turn faith to action, but they've been raised to ask themselves, "What's in it for me?" They want to get serious about the Christian life—but in a new-fashioned way that works for them.

That's why we've introduced The Christian Lifestyle Series. It's designed to help today's adults "get real" about their commitment to Christ. Each course nudges them toward becoming more consistent disciples—without browbeating or boring them. Each session helps them to be honest about their struggles and take realistic, workable steps toward greater faithfulness.

Sessions for Today's Groups

Whether you lead a large Sunday school class or a small group, you know that today's adults hate five things:
- Boring lectures
- Lots of homework
- Being told what to think
- Subjects that have nothing to do with their everyday lives; and
- Courses that seem to go on forever.

The Christian Lifestyle Series lightens the load of lecture and increases active group participation. Each course offers reproducible student Resource sheets instead of requiring group members to read time-consuming, expensive student books. Each session asks for and respects group members' contributions and emphasizes real-life application. And instead of lasting twelve or thirteen weeks, each course wraps up in seven. If you want to fit a quarterly thirteen-week format, just combine two courses and skip the introductory session in one of them.

Format for Today's Leaders

Because you're busy, these sessions are easy to prepare and use. The step-by-step plans are easy to follow; instructions to the leader are in regular type, things you might say aloud are in bold type, and suggested answers are in parentheses.

A helpful article introduces the course, giving you an overview of the topic. The reproducible student Resource sheets are meant to be photocopied and handed out—or turn some into overhead projector transparencies if you like. Most sessions include a Resource sheet that will help prepare group members for your next meeting, too.

As always, feel free to adapt this course to the needs of your group. And may God use these sessions to help your group members discover the joy of a truly Christian lifestyle.

Ardith Bradford, Series Editor

USING PEOPLE'S GIFTS

By Don Cousins

Having grown up in a strong evangelical church, I was privileged to receive solid biblical teaching for the first eighteen years of my life. So it seems strange to even admit to you that I didn't hear about spiritual gifts until I went away to college.

During my freshman year I received a long letter from a friend. It contained a thorough description and explanation of the spiritual gifts. After reading the material, I had two immediate and almost simultaneous reactions. The first was *"Wow—what a great concept! Every believer has been given a divine ability to make a difference in God's kingdom. This is revolutionary! If this were incorporated and practiced in every church in America today, what a difference it would make!"* My second thought was, *"Why haven't I heard of this before? I can't believe that I've sat for eighteen years in a Bible-teaching church and never really heard anything about this. It's unbelievable!"*

Yet, as unbelievable as that was—and still is—to me, it was true. I had never received an explanation of the spiritual gifts, much less seen their application in the church. Although I didn't realize it at that time, this new understanding would greatly impact my future life and ministry. Let me explain.

During that freshman year of college, I decided to pursue a career in ministry. I returned home to the Chicagoland area and joined my old friend Bill Hybels, and a handful of other people, in planting Willow Creek Community Church. For seventeen years I served on the staff at Willow Creek, a church well known for its unwavering commitment to reaching unsaved people with the Gospel. Though Willow Creek has received significant attention for its evangelistic effectiveness, it should receive equal attention for its unwavering commitment to "gift-based" ministry.

At a mid-80s leadership retreat, some of us evaluated the church. We unanimously agreed that our volunteer staff was one of the church's three greatest strengths. Why? What had caused that? *Spiritual Gifts!* Our people had discovered and were exercising their spiritual gifts. The result? A divinely empowered volunteer army for God. That's what they were and, for that matter, still are. In fact, it's no exaggeration to say that Willow Creek would not be the church it is today were it not for the volunteers who make it run. Thousands, literally thousands, of them are making a difference for God.

Valuing People's Gifts

From day one, we placed a value on helping believers discover their divine giftedness and find a place where they could contribute according to that giftedness. The result has been multifaceted. First of all, those believers are bearing fruit—making a difference in building the body of Christ. Secondly, they are fulfilled. They walk around with a joy in their hearts and a sense of deep satisfaction in their gut, knowing that what they are doing really matters, really counts, and is making a difference. Thirdly, they are faithful over time. They keep serving—year, after year, after year. In fact, the church has more problems with people burning out due to over-involvement than it does with people saying, "I've grown tired of this," "I don't want to do it anymore," or "This bores me."

And so, the impact has been fruitfulness, personal fulfillment, and faithfulness. And isn't that our goal—to see all believers being *fruitful, fulfilled,* and *faithful* over time in their service for God? Oh, if only every believer knew those three "f's," our churches would be different places today.

Putting People to Work

Well, the result at Willow Creek has been that volunteer army, but more than that. You see, in addition to that volunteer army, the impact of spiritual giftedness has been the development of the paid staff. You ask, "What do you mean?" Well, I mean that the majority of the non-clerical staff at Willow Creek are homegrown—they have been raised up from within the congregation. How? Let me explain.

Many people, while employed elsewhere, got a taste of what it meant to be used of God in the church. Their gifts were identified and they began to exercise them. Those gifts were empowered by the Holy Spirit, and the result was a divine sort of impact. In many cases, people reacted to that impact with "We want more of this!" And they went for it. The more they tasted of difference-making, the more they *wanted* to taste of it. After all, no thrill surpasses the thrill of seeing God use our lives to make a difference.

Well, as Bill, other key church leaders, and I watched God's work going on through some of these people, we would say to each other, "We need to give these people jobs (as secretaries, graphic designers, program coordinators, etc.) so they can do this more often. They're making an incredible impact in five, ten, or fifteen hours a week, but just think if they had forty or fifty hours a week through which to really employ their gifts!" And so, in many cases, we went to them and said, "We'd like to give you an office, a salary, and a job description that allows you to use your gift full time."

Although this may sound exaggerated or overly simplistic, it's really not. Spiritual gifts, when exercised under the Holy Spirit's power, create a powerful result—not only *through* the individual, but *within* the individual. So, though your church may not be large enough to offer careers to non-clerical people, you may be able to provide counsel for those who, through exercising their gifts, feel called to some full-time Christian ministry.

As I look back on my seventeen-year involvement at Willow Creek, I count it a great privilege to have been a part of establishing a value—to see as many people as possible get a taste for gift-based ministry. The impact has been divine.

Making a Difference

Now my final words are to you, the leader of these seven sessions on spiritual gifts. Don't underestimate the significance of your role—many of the people who will sit around you in the weeks to come are in the dark concerning God's gifting for them. While they've heard many good messages, many may be ignorant or confused about the role of spiritual gifts in their lives. They don't really understand what it's all about and have not yet tasted of the power of giftedness in action. And so, I challenge you to make a difference yourself. Here's how:

1. Help your people see God as an incredibly personal God. Friends, He is a personal God, and His giving us spiritual gifts is one way we know that. You see, God is so personal that He has given each of us at least one gift. First Corinthians 12:11 says, "All these [gifts] are the work of one and the same Spirit, and he gives them to each one, just as he determines." Verse 18 says, "But in fact God has arranged the parts in the body, every one of them, just as he wanted them to be." Our God is so personal that through His Holy Spirit He assigns gifts to individual believers with the intent that they make a specific contribution to the body of

Christ. Our God is a personal God! Make it your goal to have your people *see* God that way and worship Him for being so.

2. Help your people discover their gift(s). Make this course come alive. Teach it with such passion and clarity that the people in your group actually discover their gifts and are motivated to use them. Pray over this material. Pray for the people. And pray for discernment, wisdom, and insight as it relates to each of them as individuals. Teach with enthusiasm. Explain and illustrate each gift with a relevant application. When you draw a clear picture of each gift in action, people will be able to say, "That's me!" or "That's not me." It's your job to help every person discover his or her own gift(s)!

3. Help your people find a place to try their gift(s). Like a football coach who uses a chalkboard and "X's" and "O's" to explain plays, explain the gifts. Then, like the coach, take your players to the field of play. The game's not won in the locker room; it's won on the field. Get your players on the field. It's on the field that God, others, you, and the individual have the opportunity to affirm or deny the presence of a specific gift. This means being willing to follow up each individual in your group, long after these sessions are completed.

4. Affirm your people's gift-based ministries. Watch, observe, and when they have finished their gift-based assignments, step back in. Talk with them and ask, "Did you sense God using your life for this purpose? Do you feel fulfilled? Did you enjoy it? Do you want to do it again?" At the same time, it is your task as the leader to give your objective opinion. Your honest affirmation or denial of their gifts in action is extremely important. If there's doubt in your mind and theirs, encourage them to experiment again. If there's no doubt, encourage them to continue and develop their gifts with the hope of even greater impact.

If, as a result of this study, you facilitate each person's walk through those four steps of seeing God as a personal God, discovering a specific gift, trying that gift, and then affirming it, then you have done them, the church, and God a great service. And, by the way, it's my guess that along the way you'll taste the flavor of difference-making yourself, and you'll return to taste it again and again.

WHO AM I?
Identifying Ourselves As Gifted Children of God

I am privileged to be involved in a "seeker church." From our founding, two years ago, we have sought to present Christian truth in a way people can understand. We avoid "inside lingo" that only experienced Christians understand. We explain each aspect of our worship. We try to make visitors feel very welcome.

As a result, our church is full of new believers. They may not know all the Bible verses yet, but they know Christ personally—and it's exciting to see God working in their lives.

When our pastor planned a series of sermons (and a special seminar) on spiritual gifts, I was skeptical. I had always thought, *This is a subject for more experienced Christians. Let them learn the Word for a few years first.*

But I began to realize that spiritual gifts are an important part of a new Christian's experience. This biblical teaching answers two crucial questions for a new or untrained believer: Who am I now? Where do I fit in?

So that's where we're starting this study—not with comprehensive lists of gifts, definitions, and theological debates (though we'll get to those), but with those two simple, yet profound questions that your class members may be asking too.

Where You're Headed:
To help group members see themselves as gifted children of God, with God-given, Spirit-driven abilities.

Scriptures You'll Apply:
I Corinthians 12:4-12

Things You'll Need:
- Bibles
- Copies of Resource 1, "The Christian Life and All the Rest"
- Copies of Resource 2, "Gifts Galore"
- Copies of Resource 3, "Teamwork" (optional)
- Pens or pencils
- Chalkboard and chalk or newsprint and marker
- Two actors prepared to do the skit on Resource 1

1
What Does It Mean?
(5-10 minutes)

Getting a Grip on Our Christian Identity

Start by asking, **What does it mean to be a Christian?** You might rephrase it as, **How are we who are Christians different? What do we have that others don't?** [*Write responses on the chalkboard.*] (Answers might include eternal life with God; a relationship with God; love, joy, peace, and other fruits of the Spirit; spiritual gifts; purpose in life; etc.)

Have someone read II Corinthians 5:17. **What happens when we are "in Christ"?** (We are "new creations." God actually re-makes us.) **What does He change in us? What does He re-create?** (Some of the same answers apply here, but it's a new way of looking at it. God remakes our priorities, our attitudes, our desires. But here's something else: He gives us empowered abilities—spiritual gifts that enable us to do new things for His glory.)

2
Vacation or Adventure
(5-10 minutes)

Exploring Two Strategies of the Christian Life

Sometimes we focus on all the things we get as believers. But one of the best things God gives us is the ability to give back to Him.

The skit on Resource 1, "The Christian Life and all the Rest," may help. You should have two actors prepared to do this drama. Introduce them now.

After the drama, talk about it. **What was the difference between the two characters?** (Obviously, one was excited and the other was relaxed. One seemed like a new Christian, the other more experienced.) **With which character do you most closely identify?** Answers will vary, but it's important to get people thinking about their own Christian experience. Do they feel something is missing, etc.? Surfacing such feelings will help motivate them for this series of studies.

In what way is the Christian life a "vacation"? (The character mentioned several points. Jesus gives us rest and peace. For people who are in turmoil, Christ gives their souls a break.) **How can the Christian life be an "adventure" for us?** (Probably by getting more involved in doing God's work—and using our gifts to do so.)

This is an important point, so make it strongly: **God does not just offer us rest and peace, He offers fulfillment. He gives us something important to do.**

He does not offer a vacation from our troubles, but an adventure through them. He equips each of us for a special task, and empowers us to do it.

3
Present Company
(15-20 minutes)

Looking at the Bible's Picture of a Gifted Church

Hand out Resource 2, "Gifts Galore." **To give a fresh flavor to a familiar passage, this sheet contains a paraphrase of I Corinthians 12:4-12.** Give group members a few minutes to read the text and answer the questions. Then talk through it.

1. What things are described as "different" in this passage? (Kinds of gifts; ways of serving; jobs to do.)

2. What things are "the same"? (The Spirit; the Master; God.)

3. Who receives "a present" from the Spirit? (Each person who is a Christian.) This is an important point: *Every Christian* **has a gift from the Spirit. It may or may not be one of the gifts listed in this passage, but the Bible teaches that each believer is specially gifted by God.**

4. Why are these "presents" given? ("For everyone's good." That is, everyone in the church. Gifts are not for our personal well-being, but for the building up of the church and God's glory.)

5. What spiritual gifts are listed here? (A message of wisdom, a message of knowledge, faith, healing, miracles, prophetic messages, discernment, tongues, interpretation of tongues.) Explain that you'll be exploring the specific gifts in later sessions. This list seems to contain all the *spectacular* gifts; other texts list more *common* gifts like teaching, leadership, encouragement, and hospitality.

[Note: Don't get embroiled in a discussion on whether the "supernatural" gifts are for today. You'll have time for that in Session 6. For now, you might say that it's likely that these more unusual gifts were emphasized in Corinth because of unique circumstances in that church and city.]

6. How does the Spirit decide who gets what? (He gives "just as He pleases.") We do not earn our gifts. They are given from the pure grace of God.

Based on this passage, we might think of the church as a class for gifted children. So we might think of ourselves as "gifted children."

4
Beyond Talent
(5-10 minutes)

Considering the Difference between Spiritual Gifts and Natural Talents

Are spiritual gifts the same as natural talents? If someone has a flair for drawing, singing, or speaking, we say, "That's a gift." Is that what we're talking about here? (No.) **What's the difference?** As people answer, group responses into the following chart, which you'll write on the chalkboard.

Natural Talents	Spiritual Gifts
Given by God at birth	Given by God at *re*birth
Physical or mental ability	Physical or mental ability coupled with spiritual desire
Ability develops with natural human growth	Ability develops with spiritual growth
For use in the world or church	For use in the church

Some additional points to consider:

• **There is nothing wrong with natural talents.** They are also God-given, and we can use them to glorify God. But spiritual gifts are something special. They relate to our function with the church—the body of Christ that ministers to one another and to unbelievers.

• **God sometimes will adopt or adapt a natural talent as a spiritual gift.** For instance, one may have a natural talent for teaching. Many unbelievers do. When such a person becomes a Christian, God *may* give the spiritual gift of teaching, a special ability to teach the things of God and a discernment about how spiritual truths are getting through.

• **Natural talents may be used within the working of a spiritual gift.** One might say, "I have the spiritual gift of playing the piano." No, not exactly. That person may have a spiritual gift of encouraging, and may express it through the piano.

Ask if there are any questions, before you conclude.

5
We've Got the Power

(5-10 minutes)

Seeking the Power of God within Us

Conclude by saying something like this: **What do people in this world really want? We talked earlier about "fulfillment," and fulfillment comes when we're able to do something that really matters. But sometimes we find ourselves running around doing a lot of things that *don't* matter—and we just can't find a way to make a difference. The world is spinning beyond our control. We feel helpless. Do you feel, or have you ever felt, that way?** Share something out of your own experience first. This will break the ice and help others feel more free to talk about their personal experiences.

The wonderful thing about spiritual gifts is that God is sharing His almighty power with us. He enables us to do important things. Together with the rest of the church—His body—we are carrying out His work on earth.

If you are a Christian, you are a gifted child of God. And because of the spiritual gift He has given you—whatever that may be—you have the power to make a difference. How does that make you feel?

As you go to prayer, invite group members to tell God how they feel in a sentence or two. They may feel grateful, or pressured, or full of praise, or worried about finding their gift. Whatever, ask them to bring it to the Lord. When all who want to have prayed, close by asking God's guidance for the rest of this series.

If you'd like to prepare people for next week's session, distribute copies of Resource 3, "Teamwork," and suggest that they complete it and bring it back with them next week.

SETTING: A arrives in "the Christian life," all excited, and meets **B**, who is more serene.

A: All right, I'm a Christian. Now what?

B: What do you mean?

A: Now what? What's next? I'm eager to get to it.

B: To what?

A: That's what I'm asking. What do I do now?

B: Relax. Isn't it great just to know you're saved?

A: Yes, it is! But I feel I should be doing something about it.

B: Jesus did it all. That's the wonderful thing about grace. "Not by works, lest anyone boast."

A: I know, I know. But is that all there is, just rest?

B: Jesus has welcomed us into His rest. "All you who are weary and burdened." Now we share in His peace. It's like a vacation—a spiritual vacation we can take any time at all.

A: But I don't *want* a vacation. I want an *adventure*. I feel that God has given me something—a whole new life that I want to share in any way I can. I feel so—so powerful, like I have the power of God inside me. Does that sound crazy?

B: Well, yes.

A: Wait! Who's that over there? He's talking to people; he's caring for people. Is he a Christian too?

B: Oh, yes. He's got special gifts.

A: That's great the way he's using them! Isn't that great? I have to talk to him. Do you mind?

B: Not at all. You'd like him. He was just like you when he first got here. Full of spark and drive.

A: [*about to leave*] Well, I'll catch you later.

B: I'll be here.

A: I hope you enjoy your "vacation."

B: Thanks. I hope you enjoy your "adventure."

Gifts Galore

(BASED ON I CORINTHIANS 12:4-12)

There are different kinds of gifts, but they are all given by the same Spirit. And there are different ways of serving, but everyone serves the same Master. And there are different jobs to do, but it is the same God who is doing all those jobs in and through us all.

So each of us receives a present from the Spirit, and we are to use it for everyone's good. The Spirit gives one of us a message of wisdom, and someone else a message of knowledge. One person receives faith from the Spirit, and another receives gifts of healing. Still another is given the ability to work miracles, another can utter prophetic messages, and another can discern what kind of spirit is motivating people. One person is enabled to speak in different languages and another is enabled to interpret those languages.

But it's one and the same Spirit who makes all of these things happen. He gives each person just the kind of gift He pleases.

1. What things are described as "different" in this passage?

2. What things are "the same"?

3. Who receives "a present" from the Spirit?

4. Why are these "presents" given?

5. What spiritual gifts are listed here?

6. How does the Spirit decide who gets what?

TEAMWORK

During the next week—as you watch TV, read the paper or magazines, or just watch people in action at home or at work—look for examples of the following:

1. A team that includes people with different strengths:

2. A team that functions poorly because it needs someone with a certain specialty:

What specialty is needed?

3. A person who functions well in a group and helps that group do well—not because he or she is the smartest, strongest, or most talented, but because he or she has a unique gift and uses it well:

What gift is used?

WHERE DO I FIT IN?
Finding Our Place in God's Community

One of my jobs at church is leading the singles group Bible study. The group includes several brand-new believers, and it is thrilling to watch them grow. As they have discovered their own identity in Christ, they have been empowered to confront certain crises in their own lives. And they all testify to the strength they draw from the singles group itself.

In our group, we feel free to be ourselves, with all our quirks and specialties. God is working a little differently in each of us, so when we come together it's a delicious stew of Christian fellowship. Discerning, Gail cuts to the heart of every issue, while Robin flavors everything with common-sense wisdom. Deb, with quiet thoughtfulness, mixes in mercy. Lauree stirs in a servant attitude, spiced up with with clever quips. Arlen, with a jovial spirit, peppers everything with encouragement; and I blend it all together with the gift of teaching. These and others offer their gifts for the good of the group and God's glory. It is the church in microcosm, a family of the familyless, blessing and being blessed. When we meet together, we are at home.

Spiritual gifts cannot be used in isolation. They belong to the body of Christ. That's what this session is about.

Where You're Headed:
To help group members see their place in the church as using their spiritual gifts for the Body's good and for God's glory.

Scriptures You'll Apply:
I Corinthians 12:12, 27-31; Ephesians 4:11-13

Things You'll Need:
- Bibles
- Copies of Resource 4, "Body Language"
- Copies of Resource 5, "Welcomed Words" (optional)
- Pens or pencils
- Chalkboard and chalk or newsprint and marker

1
Teamwork
(10-15 minutes)

Seeing How Various Groups
Fit Their Gifts Together

Divide into groups of three to five people each. Explain: **Each group should prepare to act out a team situation. We need only about sixty seconds of drama from each of you, so it shouldn't be too involved. But it does have to have *two scenes*. In the first thirty seconds or so, we need to see this "team" trying to function without a key person—someone who possesses a speciality needed for the group to function successfully. In the second scene, that person shows up and fills the gap. If people in your group filled out and brought back Resource 3, "Teamwork," from last time, you may choose an example they observed; or you may agree on a new one.**

Give groups about five minutes to plan their sixty-second skits. Then have each group perform. Keep everything simple and nonthreatening. Have fun with it.

Afterward, discuss the dynamics of those team situations. **What "gifts" were evident? What happened when the team was not complete? Think about a personal experience with a similar team: How did you feel when part of the first type of team? when part of the second type of team?** By helping group members surface their own feelings of frustration (when part of a dysfunctional team) or enthusiasm (when part of a functional team), you can motivate them to do *their* part on *God's* team.

2
Personal Salvation?
(5 minutes)

Understanding the Corporate
Nature of Our Faith

When we who are Christians say that we've accepted Jesus as our personal Savior, what do we mean by "personal" Savior? (We mean that we have made an individual commitment to Christ. It's not just the church we go to, or the family we're in— each of us has made an individual choice to follow Jesus.)

The problem is that sometimes Christianity *remains* a personal thing. We focus on our *own* experience of Christ and forget that God works through the church as well. We go to church to get a personal blessing from the service and may actually forget that others are there too.

We must never lose the sense of personal commitment in our faith. But we must expand it to include the rest of the body of Christ. Christianity is a group faith as well as a personal faith.

Refer the group to I Corinthians 3:16. Have someone read it. **"You yourselves are God's temple." It's clear from the context that Paul was not talking about the individual bodies of believers—he talked about that later** [*see chapter 6*]**—but about the church as a whole. We together are God's temple, and God's Spirit lives in us.**

3

How the Body Works Out

(25-30 minutes)

Getting a Biblical View
of the Church in Action

Hand out copies of Resource 4, "Body Language." Give group members a few minutes to read through the text and the questions. Then ask each question, giving people a minute or two to write down their answers before discussing them:

1. How is the church like a body? (As the body has different parts with different functions, so does the church.)

Have someone read the second paraphrase (Eph. 4:11-13); then ask the second question:

2. What is the purpose of our spiritual gifts? (The NIV says "to prepare" God's people. Other versions refer to "reshaping" or "restoring" God's people.) **Let's explore this one a little further.**

The Greek word here is an interesting one, *katartizo* **(kah-tar-TIDZ-oh).** *[Write "katartizo" on the chalkboard.]* **It can mean a number of different things: to adjust, restore, repair, perfect, furnish completely. You can hear the word "art" in there.** *Artizo* *[underline this part of the word]* **is the root word, meaning to make something—to craft it or shape it—to be an artisan.** *Kata [point to this first part of the word]* **is the prefix, which at times means "down." One English comparison might be "to nail down" something. What do we mean by that?** (In one sense, it's to finish something. In another, it's to repair something that has come apart. Sometimes, when finishing an especially good project or saying an especially good thing, or hitting an especially good triple in a softball game, we might say, "I nailed it." We mean that we finished it and it was well done.)

So Paul says that our spiritual gifts are for the purpose of "nailing down" God's people.

Explore some of the biblical examples of *katartizo* with your group. Assign each passage to a volunteer and have it read before you share insights about it:

Mark 1:19—**When Jesus started calling His disciples, He found a couple of fishermen mending their nets. The word used for "mending" here is** *katartizo*: **restoring.**

Galatians 6:1—**Here Paul mentions a situation in which a Christian plunges into seriously sinful behavior. The spiritual leaders of the church, he says, should "*restore* him gently."** *Katartizo* **again.**

I Corinthians 1:10—**When he was writing to the Corinthians, who were torn apart by various controversies, Paul prayed that they would be "perfectly united [*katartizo*] in mind and thought."**

I Thessalonians 3:10—**Here Paul told another church that he wanted to be there to "supply" what was lacking in their faith. He wanted to nail down their faith.**

Hebrews 11:3; 13:21—**The writer of these passages used** *katartizo* **in two senses. First he mentions how God "formed" the world—that's** *katartizo* **in the sense of shaping or crafting (Heb. 11:3). But later he prays that God would "equip [*katartizo*] [believers] with everything good for doing his will" (Heb. 13:21).**

So God not only shapes the world, but He also shapes *us* **by**

giving us what we need to restore and shape each other. How does this restoring and shaping work in the church? The next question on our resource sheet helps us answer that.

3. **What will result as Christians use their gifts?** (Christians will *work at serving God* and *building up Christ's body.* This will help them *reach unity in faith and knowledge of Christ, become mature,* and *experience the fullness of Christ.*)

Let's consider those things more closely:

Work at serving God—If an appliance doesn't work, we need to repair it so it will do what it's supposed to. If a church doesn't work, we need to restore it, so it will once again serve God effectively. All the gifts come into play here. Many of us have known situations, at a job or perhaps at church, where we were ready to work, but we hadn't been given an assignment, or we didn't know how to do it. That's why we need administrators and teachers. We need encouragers and leaders to motivate people to work. We need servers and carers to set an example for others. We need people with gifts of hospitality and giving to support the work. With everything in place, the church can "work" again, serving God as it was originally intended to do.

Build up the Body of Christ—We're supposed to be into "body-building." Actually, the new thing is "body-shaping"—and that fits right in with *katartizo*. Of course, it's not our muscles we're developing. It's the body of Christ, which is the church. But think about it. A well-shaped body is in balance; all its members are contributing equally to its health. It is getting proper nourishment and exercise. So it is with the body of Christ. We need to be in balance, getting proper nutrition, with all members exercising their gifts. Some churches have "stars" who seem more important than everyone else. That's not healthy. It's like the guy who has great biceps but flabby legs. It's out of balance.

Reach unity in faith and knowledge of Christ—Part of the perfection we want to nail down for the church is its unity. There are so many controversies that threaten to divide us. But as we use our gifts, we can be united in the service of one Lord.

Become mature—Who wants to get old? Well, kids do. They long for the days when they will be big enough, smart enough, responsible enough to do what they really want to do. The Bible frequently talks about the Christian life as a growth process. We come into God's family as babies and we grow into maturity. Youthful energy and abandon give way to wisdom.

Experience the fullness of Christ—There is so much that Christ can give us! We haven't even scratched the surface. But as we use our gifts and grow together, we are headed in the right direction. More and more of Christ's love and wisdom fill our lives.

Paul lived in a time, not unlike ours, when people were offering easy answers for instant spirituality. "Fullness" was a key buzzword.

Everyone, it seems, wants a fuller spiritual experience. If you can get it overnight—go for it! But Paul says that the true fullness of Christ is a growth thing. We grow into it, and we grow together into it. It's not this person or that one suddenly "attaining" a higher level of oneness with the divine. It's all of us helping each other along toward the spiritual riches of Jesus Christ.

Now turn to that final question:

4. What gifts are listed in these two passages? (Corinthians lists apostles, prophets, teachers, miracle-workers, healers, helpers, administrators, and people who could speak in tongues. Ephesians adds evangelists and pastor-teachers.)

In the next few weeks you'll be digging into the individual gifts. But for now get the point across that Scripture has several different lists of gifts. Some gifts are listed two or three times, others just once. Different gifts seem to be required for different churches in different situations.

4
Last Words
(5-10 minutes)

Realizing We Have a
Place in the Body

Conclude by asking: **So how do you feel now? Not only do you have an *identity* as a gifted child of God, and the *power* to do significant things with the gift you've been given, but you also have a *place* in which to use that gift. You are part of a family, part of a *body*. What you do affects others. You are responsible to them and for them, and they are responsible for you. How does that make you feel?** (Look for their honest responses—gratefulness, warmth, pressure, purpose, defensiveness—whatever.)

Invite everyone to join in the closing prayer, telling God how they feel about what they've learned today. Close by thanking God for living in His body, the church.

If you'd like to prepare people for the next session, hand out copies of Resource 5, "Welcomed Words," for them to consider during the week.

BODY LANGUAGE

I Corinthians 12:12, 27-31

The body is a unit, though it is made up of many parts; and though all its parts are many, they form one body. So it is with Christ. . . . Now you are the body of Christ, and each one of you is a part of it. And in the church God has appointed first of all apostles, second prophets, third teachers, then workers of miracles, also those having gifts of healing, those able to help others, those with gifts of administration, and those speaking in different kinds of tongues. Are all apostles? Are all prophets? Are all teachers? Do all work miracles? Do all have gifts of healing? Do all speak in tongues? Do all interpret? But eagerly desire the greater gifts.

Ephesians 4:11-13

It was he who gave some to be apostles, some to be prophets, some to be evangelists, and some to be pastors and teachers, to prepare God's people for works of service, so that the body of Christ may be built up until we all reach unity in the faith and in the knowledge of the Son of God and become mature, attaining to the whole measure of the fullness of Christ.

1. How is the church like a body?

2. What is the purpose of our spiritual gifts?

3. What will result as Christians use their gifts?

4. What gifts are listed in these two passages?

WELCOMED WORDS

This week, think about two people who have ministered to you through their speaking. They might be preachers, teachers, or just friends who seemed to know the right thing to say.

1. Name:

_____

Briefly, what was one thing this person said to help you?

2. Name:

_____

Briefly, what was one thing this person said to help you?

How do these two people compare with each other in the *way* they speak and in what they say?

WHAT CAN I SAY?
Unwrapping the Speaking Gifts

Think of the people who have been the most influential in your spiritual life. Who motivated you to give your life to Christ? Who inspired you to deepen that commitment? Who made things clear to you? Who encouraged and strengthened you during tough times?

Whether pastors, missionaries, teachers, or friends, those who helped you were probably using one of the spiritual gifts we're calling "speaking" gifts. Those are the gifts we'll be talking about today.

Some of your students probably have some of these gifts. It is your privilege today to help them understand those gifts and perhaps claim them as their own.

Where You're Headed:
To help group members understand the eight scriptural "speaking" gifts and to begin to determine whether they have any of these gifts.

Scriptures You'll Apply:
Primarily Romans 12:6-8; I Corinthians 12:8-10, 28-30; Ephesians 4:11; I Peter 4:9-11

Things You'll Need:
- Bibles
- Copies of Resource 6, "Gift Designation"
- Copies of Resource 7, "Speaking Gifts—I"
- Copies of Resource 8, "Speaking Gifts—II"
- Copies of Resource 9, "Whose Serve?" (optional)
- Pens and pencils
- Chalkboard and chalk or newsprint and marker

1
Silence Is Golden
(5 minutes)

Learning Just How Precious
Speaking Can Be

Write on the chalkboard "NO TALKING!" As people arrive, greet them with a wave; then point to the chalkboard message. Do your best to communicate with your group via sign language, pictures, and so on. Start to express how God has given different kinds of gifts—speaking, serving, and sign gifts. Point back to the chalkboard message whenever anyone starts to talk out loud.

Soon you and everyone else will be frustrated by this charade. Break the silence by saying: **See how important speaking is? Where would we be without it?**

Ask the group how they felt during those minutes of silence. It was fun at first, but then maybe it got frustrating. **What would it be like to do a whole session like that? There are some ideas that just require words.**

Some of the gifts God gives to believers involve speaking— proclaiming God's Word, explaining it, or encouraging some- one. These are crucial gifts. God has often used language to do His work, and with these gifts He now uses our speech for His purposes.

2
Gift List
(10-15 minutes)

Compiling the Bible's
Collection of Spiritual Gifts

Have the group turn to I Peter 4:10, 11, and ask someone to read it aloud. **What two kinds of gifts are referred to here?** (Speaking and serving.) Write these two categories on the chalk- board as two of three column headings. **We're going to find various gifts listed in Scripture. We can group them in these two categories, plus one other—"sign" gifts, for those miraculous gifts that serve as indications that God was working among His people.** Write "SIGN" on the board as the third category heading.

Think about this for a moment. When Jesus was on earth, what did He do? (He taught and preached, using His *speaking* ability to communicate truths about God's kingdom. He *served* people—remember how He washed His disciples' feet. And many of His healings were motivated by a compassion for suffering people. Yet other healings were more for effect—*signs* about His own identity. There were other miracles as well—changing water to wine, walking on the water, calming the storm. Those demon- strations of power showed the people who He was.)

What did we learn last time about the church? How did Paul describe the church, with its various parts? (As a body—the body of Christ.)

If we take that a step further, we see that the church actually carries on Christ's ministry. We speak His words, we serve in His name, and there are even manifestations of God's power that show that God is present with us. [Note: We'll deal with specific questions regarding the sign gifts in Session 5. But God does show His power through the church today—with these gifts or without them.] **We represent the physical presence of Christ on earth today. With our spiritual gifts, we do His work.**

Now begin to fill in the chart on the board. **We find one gift in I Peter 4:9, next to the verses we just read. What is that gift and**

what category would you put it in? (Hospitality; it's a serving gift.)

Hand out Resource 6, "Gift Designation," and divide into four subgroups. Assign the following Scriptures:

1. Ephesians 4:11
2. Romans 12:6-8
3. I Corinthians 12:8-10
4. I Corinthians 12:28-30

Read through the assigned passage and find the gifts listed there. Then decide which category each gift belongs in. If you finish before I call time, start working on one of the other Scripture passages. Allow a few minutes for group study, then call for reports. As reporters identify each gift and its category, write it on the chalkboard chart. Participants should also complete their charts on Resource 6 as they listen to each report.

1. Ephesians 4:11—(Apostles, prophets, evangelists, pastors, and teachers all belong in the speaking gifts category.)

2. Romans 12:6-8—(Prophesying is a speaking gift [already mentioned in Ephesians 4:11]; serving is a serving gift, of course [we'll call it "helping"]; teaching and encouraging are both speaking gifts; contributing [or "giving"], leadership, and mercy are all serving gifts.)

3. I Corinthians 12:8-10—(We'll loosely classify wisdom and knowledge under speaking gifts ["the message of . . ."]; faith is a serving gift; healing and miracles are sign gifts; prophecy [already mentioned] is a speaking gift; distinguishing between spirits [or "discernment"] we'll call a serving gift; tongues and interpretation of tongues are sign gifts.)

4. I Corinthians 12:28-30—(This is much like the Ephesians text. Apostles, prophets, and teachers have speaking gifts. Miracles and healing are sign gifts. Helping and administration are serving gifts. Tongues is a sign gift.)

The final chart should look something like this:

Speaking Gifts	Serving Gifts	Sign Gifts
Apostleship	Hospitality	Healing
Prophecy	Helping	Miracles
Evangelism	Giving	Tongues
Pastoring	Leadership	Interpretation
(Shepherding)	Mercy	of Tongues
Teaching	Faith	
Encouraging	Discernment	
Wisdom	Administration	
Knowledge		

[Note: There's nothing inspired about this particular classification. Some people might disagree about where to put which gift. This is the arrangement we'll be following for this course of study.]

Someone may ask if God gives other spiritual gifts in addition to those listed here. You can say that the Bible doesn't tell us whether this is an exhaustive list. In this course, we'll focus on the twenty gifts we have listed, yet allow for the idea that God may give other gifts as well. Here's why: the fact that there are three or four different gift lists in Scripture (and those don't match) indicates that Paul was not working from some divinely dictated master list. God seemed to work with different churches in different ways, perhaps according to the unique needs of those places. Also, we see examples of God enabling believers in unique ways through history and in Scripture. Some scholars have made strong cases for additional gifts; such as creative communication, craftsmanship, counseling, prayer, worship, martyrdom, and celibacy. We'll focus on the less controversial gifts clearly listed in Scripture. If someone is convinced that he or she does not have any of the twenty gifts listed, then you can start talking about the extrabiblical gifts.

3
Speak Up
(25-30 minutes)

Examining the Specific
Speaking Gifts

Today we're going to take a closer look at the eight speaking gifts, investigating certain Scriptures that may help us. Hand out Resources 7 and 8, "Speaking Gifts—I" and "Speaking Gifts—II." Depending on the size of your class and the time you have to spend, assign each gift to an individual, a pair, or a subgroup. You might use the same four subgroups used in Step 2 and have each group research two gifts. Using the verses listed, researchers need to find out as much as they can about each gift, *defining it* and figuring out *how to use it*. Those who finish first can move on to another gift of their choice.

Allow about ten minutes for study. Then go through the gifts one at a time, with everyone taking notes as each report is given.

1. Apostleship

Does apostleship apply only to the Twelve (and Paul)? (It seemed to have a specialized use for the Twelve and an expanded use for other church leaders, such as Paul, Barnabas, and James the brother of Jesus [Acts 14:14; Gal. 1:19]. It may also have had a general use for any missionary ["messenger"] sent out by a church [Phil. 2:25].)

Job description: (A herald who teaches true faith to people who need to hear it [I Tim. 2:7]; one who crosses cultural lines to present the Gospel in understandable ways [I Cor. 9:19-23].)

Qualities: ("Set apart" and sent by God [Acts 13:2, 3]; able to preach [Rom. 10:15]; adaptable to different cultures [I Cor. 9:19-23].)

What role might a person with the expanded form of this gift have in the church today? (Missionary, leader of evangelistic efforts, or church planter.)

2. Prophecy

Does prophecy apply only to predicting future events? (No. In biblical times it included prediction [Acts 21:10, 11], but it also included insightful proclamation of God's truth [Acts 15:32].)

Job description: (A prophet proclaims God's truth in such a way that believers are encouraged, strengthened, and comforted

[Rom. 12:6; I Cor. 14:1-4].)

Qualities: (Biblical prophets seemed to be bold, willing to confront problem areas, but also eager to support the faithful.)

What role might a person with this gift have in the church today? (Preacher or writer.)

3. Evangelism

What can we learn about evangelism from the experience of "Philip the evangelist"? (Evangelism is sometimes accompanied by great power, sometimes quiet explanation; the Lord guides it [Acts 8:5, 26-40].)

Content: (The good news of salvation which brings peace [Acts 10:36; 17:18].)

Job description: (An evangelist has a passion for the good news of Christ and expresses it wherever possible; wins people, but also strengthens and encourages them to remain true to God [Acts 14:21, 22].)

Qualities: (An evangelist is concerned for the eternal situation of others; is level-headed and able to endure hardships [II Tim. 4:5].)

What role might a person with this gift have in the church today? (Pastor, teacher, youth leader, outreach leader, missionary, visitation team member, or layperson who keeps drawing people into the faith.)

4. Pastoring

What can "shepherds" learn from Jesus' example? (The Good Shepherd cares for His flock's well-being and gives sacrificially of Himself [John 10:11, 14, 15]—so do "under-shepherds.")

Job description: (Must teach and care for the spiritual well-being of God's people [I Tim. 3:2; I Pet. 5:1-3].)

Qualities: (Must be able to teach—have knowledge of the Word and good communication skills; must have good character—not be greedy; must be responsible, respectable, mature, eager to serve, exemplary [I Tim. 3:1-7; I Pet. 5:1-3].)

What role might a person with this gift have in the church today? (Pastor, counselor, elder, or layperson who's active in spiritual leadership and caregiving.)

5. Teaching

How did Apollos, Priscilla, and Aquila use their teaching gifts? (Apollos spoke boldly and accurately, but with limited knowledge; Priscilla and Aquila taught Apollos privately [Acts 18:24-28].)

Adding Acts 20:20, 21; Hebrews 5:11-13; and James 3:1, what can we learn about a teacher's content, job description, and qualities?

Content: (The need for repentance and faith; sometimes basic, but sometimes more mature aspects of discerning good and evil; the "word of Christ.")

Job description: (Communicating God's truth in a way people can understand and apply it.)

Qualities: (Public or private; mature—able to understand the "meat" of God's Word; held to a higher standard; wise.)

What role might a person with this gift have in the church today? (Teacher, Bible study leader, small group facilitator.)

6. Encouraging

What helpful hints about encouraging can we pick up from the Holy Spirit's ministry? (Encouraging involves teaching and reminding others of Christ's teaching and identity [John 14:26, 27; 15:26, 27].)

Who was the best biblical example of someone with this gift? (Barnabas [Acts 4:16].)

What can we learn from him about encouragement? (We should give people a chance and help them use their gifts; we should affirm and motivate them. For example, Barnabas took Paul to the apostles; encouraged (with Paul) the churches they ministered to; stood up for John Mark [Acts 9:26, 27; 13:43; 14:20b-22; 15:37-39].)

Job description: (Strengthen other believers by building them up and reminding them of God's eternal support [Heb. 10:25; I Thess. 5:11, 14].)

What role might a person with this gift have in the church today? (Such people are good in many roles: as formal or informal advisers to church leaders, as counselors and teachers, especially as youth leaders and Sunday school teachers.)

7. Wisdom

Who was an early example of someone with this gift? (Stephen [Acts 6:3, 8-10].)

How did he demonstrate this gift? (His arguments before the Sanhedrin were convincing [Acts 6:9b, 10].)

How is God's wisdom described in I Corinthians 2:6-13? (God's wisdom is different from human wisdom—it often appears foolish and unimpressive to the secular world.)

From passages already read, plus II Peter 3:15 and 16, what qualities does a person gifted with wisdom possess? (In tune with God and His principles; sometimes a convincing debater, but sometimes misunderstood.)

What role might a person with this gift have in the church today? (Administrator, counselor, leader, financial or other type of adviser.)

8. Knowledge

We see a seemingly supernatural use of this gift in Acts 5:1-11. How was it used? (The Spirit enabled Peter to know that Ananias and Sapphira were lying. God may still give people insight into the behavior and motives of others.)

Consult I Corinthians 2:10b-16; II Corinthians 11:6; Colossians 2:2, 3. How would you describe a Christian who has this gift? (In general, we can speak of this gift as an awareness of the things of God, perhaps involving knowledge of Scripture.)

What role might a person with this gift have in the church

today? (This gift can function in many areas, especially teaching and writing.)

(Note: If necessary, clarify the difference between having *knowledge* and having *wisdom*. Knowledge has to do with facts—*knowing* the truth; wisdom is the ability to *apply* that knowledge to specific situations or problems.)

4
Take One
(5-10 minutes)

Considering Any Special
Interest in Certain Gifts

Might any of these gifts belong to you? As we have talked about them, did any jump out at you as one that really interests you? If so, great! If not, don't despair. We won't be exploring *how* to find your spiritual gift until Session 6; and we still have the serving and sign gifts to talk about.

Encourage group members to consider this week whether they may have any of the speaking gifts. Then, if they want to begin exploring the *serving* gifts, which will be discussed next time, distribute copies of Resource 9, "Whose Serve?"

Close in prayer, thanking God for the gifts He has given, and asking for wisdom in this process of learning about and identifying spiritual gifts.

GIFT DESIGNATION

Read through your assigned passage and find the spiritual gifts listed there. Decide which category each gift belongs in, and write it in the appropriate box.

1. Ephesians 4:11
2. Romans 12:6-8
3. I Corinthians 12:8-10
4. I Corinthians 12:28-30

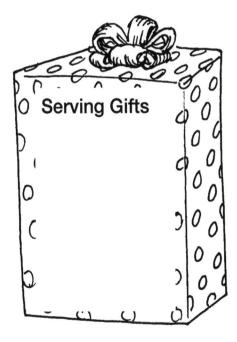

SPEAKING GIFTS—1

APOSTLESHIP • PROPHECY • EVANGELISM • PASTORING

1. Apostleship

Note: The Greek word for apostle means "sent one."

Does *apostleship* apply only to the Twelve (and Paul)? (Acts 14:14; Galatians 1:19; Philippians 2:25—"messenger" is the same Greek word.)   ☐ yes   ☐ no

Job description (I Timothy 2:7; I Corinthians 9:19-23):

Qualities (Acts 13:2, 3; Romans 10:15; I Corinthians 9:19-23):

What role might a person with the expanded form of this gift have in the church today?

2. Prophecy

Note: The Greek word means "speaking forth" or "speaking in advance."

Does *prophecy* apply only to predicting future events? (See Acts 21:10 and 11; but also Acts 15:32.)   ☐ yes   ☐ no

Job description (above passages, plus Romans 12:6 and I Corinthians 14:1-4):

Qualities:

What role might a person with this gift have in the church today?

3. Evangelism

Note: The Greek word means "reporting good news."

What can we learn about evangelism from the experience of "Philip the evangelist" (Acts 8:5, 26-40)?

In Acts 10:36 and 17:18 the word translated "preaching" is really the Greek word for "evangelizing." What does this tell us about evangelism's content?

Adding Acts 14:21, 22 and II Timothy 4:5, what can we say about a job description and qualities of an evangelist?

Job description:

Qualities:

What role might a person with this gift have in the church today?

4. Pastoring

Note: The Greek word carries the idea of "shepherding."

What can "shepherds" learn from Jesus' example (John 10:11, 14, 15)?

In I Timothy 3:1-7, Paul speaks of the church office of "overseer" or "elder." This obviously involved pastoring. From that passage and I Peter 5:1-3, what job description and necessary qualities can you discover?

Job description:

Qualities:

What role might a person with this gift have in the church today?

Speaking Gifts—II

Teaching • Encouraging • Wisdom • Knowledge

5. Teaching

How did Apollos, Priscilla, and Aquila use their teaching gifts? (Acts 18:24-28)

Adding Acts 20:20, 21; Hebrews 5:11-13; and James 3:1, what can we learn about a teacher's content, job description, and qualities?

Content:

Job description:

Qualities:

What role might a person with this gift have in the church today?

6. Encouraging

Note: The Greek verb crudely means "to be called alongside." In its noun form it is essentially the same word Jesus used for the Holy Spirit.

What helpful hints about encouraging others can we pick up from the Holy Spirit's ministry? (John 14:26, 27; 15:26, 27)

Who was the best biblical example of someone with this gift? (Acts 4:36)

What can we learn from him about encouragement? (Acts 9:26, 27; 13:43; 14:20b-22; 15:37-39)

Adding Hebrews 10:25 and I Thessalonians 5:11, 14, what job description would you come up with for an encourager?

What role might a person with this gift have in the church today?

SPEAKING GIFTS—II (CONT.)

7. Wisdom

Who was an early example of someone with this gift? (Acts 6—note especially verses 3, 8-10)

How did he demonstrate this gift? (Acts 6:9b, 10)

How is God's wisdom described in I Corinthians 2:6-13?

From passages already read, plus II Peter 3:15 and 16, what qualities does a gifted person possess?

What role might a person with this gift have in the church today?

8. Knowledge

We see a seemingly supernatural use of this gift in Acts 5:1-11. How was it used?

Consult I Corinthians 2:10b-16; II Corinthians 11:6; Colossians 2:2, 3. How would you describe a Christian who has this gift?

What role might a person with this gift have in the church today?

WHOSE SERVE?

This week, think about two people who have ministered to you through their *serving*. That is, in some way they have met your needs—maybe at a critical time or maybe just in general.

1. Name: _____
   Briefly, what was one thing this person did to help you?

2. Name: _____
   Briefly, what was one thing this person did to help you?

How do these two people compare with each other in the *way* they served?

WHAT CAN I DO?
Opening Up the Serving Gifts

"**T**oo many chiefs and not enough Indians." How many times have you heard a chaotic situation described in that way? The strength of any organization is always in its rank and file, the grass roots, the many servants. Walk into a well-run business and you will find the everyday employees working diligently, even cheerfully. But if chaos reigns among the executives, it filters down to the laborers and, ultimately, affects the quality and quantity of work.

In God's plan, His church should always have enough servants. First, by Christ's example, church leaders are to be *servant*-leaders, serving the people's needs. Second, God has given many people in the church special *serving* gifts. Look around today and appreciate those gifted people who work heartily each week for the good of the church and God's glory.

Where You're Headed:
To help group members understand the eight scriptural "serving" gifts and begin to determine whether they have any of them.

Scriptures You'll Apply:
Primarily Romans 12:6-8; I Corinthians 12:8-10, 28-30; I Peter 4:9-11

Things You'll Need:
- Bibles
- Resource 10, "Serving Gifts—I"
- Resource 11, "Serving Gifts—II"
- Resource 12, "Looking for Signs" (optional)
- Pens or pencils
- Chalkboard and chalk or newsprint and marker

1
A Job to Do
(5 minutes)

Choose three volunteers. Send two out of the room. Say this to the third: **I'm going to give the three of you a task to do. It won't be hard, but it's very important for *you* to be in charge. Don't let anyone else tell you what to do. And you must not do any work yourself. It's your job to oversee the work of the others. If you exert yourself in any way, it would be a very bad precedent. *You* are the boss; get *them* to do the work. And another thing: Don't tell the others what I've told you here. Don't tell them that you're the boss. *Show* them by the way you boss them around.**

Send that person out of the room and bring in the other two, one at a time. Say the same thing to each of them. Then bring all three back into the room and give them a task—perhaps setting up a row of chairs or distributing papers to everyone in the group.

Take a fourth person from the group aside and quietly say: **You need to enter this situation as a servant. It is your job to do what anyone tells you.** Then, after giving the three "bosses" a minute or two to lock horns, send the servant in. In moments, the job should be done.

Talk about what happened: **Why wasn't the job getting done at first?** (Obviously, no one was serving. Each thought he or she was the boss.) **When did things begin to happen?** (When the servant entered the scene.) **In what ways does this sort of thing happen in the church?** (It's possible that some churches are filled with people who want to lead instead of follow; but in our fast-paced world, it's more likely that churches have problems coming up with enough people who want to be leaders *or* followers—many are satisfied just to be spectators.)

Today, we'll be looking at the *serving* gifts—from leadership and administration, to giving and hospitality. When these gifts, along with all the other gifts, are working together, we have a properly working church—one that accomplishes God's goals with enthusiasm and joy.

2
Gift List Review
(5 minutes)

Ask people to recall the eight *speaking* gifts discussed last time. As people name them, write each gift in one column on a chalkboard or sheet of newsprint. Then see if they can remember the eight *serving* gifts. (Send them hunting in Romans 12 and I Corinthians 12, if you like.) Write these on the board in a second column.

Your lists should look like this.

Speaking Gifts	Serving Gifts
Apostleship	Hospitality
Prophecy	Helping
Evangelism	Giving
Pastoring	Leadership
Teaching	Mercy
Encouraging	Faith
Wisdom	Discernment
Knowledge	Administration

3
Gifts or Com- mands?

(5 minutes)

Considering the
Unique Responsibility
of Spiritual Gifts

Pointing to the lists on the chalkboard, say: **Aren't these gifts for everybody? Sure, some of the gifts, like apostleship or pastoring, are given to only a few. But something like evangelism—aren't we all supposed to evangelize? Today we'll be talking about serving others and showing mercy and giving to the church. Shouldn't we all be doing these things? Then what's the big deal about these gifts?** (Yes, we are all called to do some of these things. But there are some people who are given special ability and special desire in certain areas. They can provide leadership or modeling for the rest of us.)

Ask for or give examples of this happening in your own church family. Perhaps someone in the church comes to mind who is gifted in a certain area—someone who inspires others. For instance, perhaps you know someone whose gift is giving. By contributing generously and cheerfully, that person (by example) inspires others to do the same. Or perhaps you want to show mercy to someone in need, but you know your resources and abilities are very limited. So you seek the help of someone who has the gift of mercy. In doing so, you actually show mercy by finding someone else in the church who can do it better than you can. Same with evangelism. You may know someone who talks to many people about Jesus. Evangelism is second nature to that person, while it's hard for you. So you participate in evangelism by introducing an unsaved friend to a gifted evangelist who can eventually lead him or her to Christ. That's not a cop-out; it's the working of the Body.

Serving gifts are vital to the church. So let's take a closer look at each one.

4
Service Merchan- dise

(1-2 minutes)

Examining the Specific
Serving Gifts

Give everyone a pencil and a copy of Resources 10 and 11, "Serving Gifts—I" and "Serving Gifts—II." Depending on the size of your class and the time available, assign individuals, pairs, or groups one or two gifts each. **Using the verses listed, find out as much as you can about each gift, *defining it* and figuring out *how to use it.***

Allow about ten minutes for study, then call for reports, As reports are given, the rest of the class should take notes on their copies of Resources 10 and 11.

1. Hospitality
From examples in Acts 16:14, 15 and Romans 16:5, 23, what forms does hospitality in action take? (Inviting the church to meet in one's home; inviting guests for a meal or to stay the night.)

How does I Peter 4:9 say hospitality is to be extended? (Without grumbling.)

Hospitality is a requirement for church leaders (I Tim. 3:2; Titus 1:8). Why would it be so important for these people? (As church leaders, they might need to house visiting preachers or needy church members. Also, it exemplifies an open heart, necessary for church leadership.)

From the Scriptures you've read so far, plus Hebrews 13:1-3 and Romans 12:13, how would you define the spiritual gift of hospitality? (The ability to make people feel at home, whether in your own home or in a public setting. For example, certain natural "greeters" demonstrate hospitality at home, at church, or wherever they are by always making visitors feel very welcome.)

What role might a person with this gift have in the church today? (Though everyone should welcome others, some people are especially gifted for being greeters or hosts or hostesses for youth group functions or visiting missionaries, choirs, and speakers.)

2. Helping

The Bible includes several strong examples of helping (Romans 16:1, 2; Acts 9:36-40; Luke 8:1-3; Mark 15:40, 41). What did these people do to help? (Phoebe helped the Cenchrea church. And though this passage doesn't say so specifically, she probably supported Paul financially and may have helped in making contacts for him or arranging details for some of his travels [Rom. 16:1, 2]. Tabitha [Dorcas] helped by making clothes for the poor and caring for their needs [Acts 9:36-40]. The women of Jesus' ministry also helped financially, and possibly with logistical matters of Jesus' travels—food and lodging [Luke 8:1-3; Mark 15:40, 41].)

From your study so far, and I Peter 4:10 and 11, how would you define the biblical gift of serving/helping? (Providing practical assistance to others in the church, and doing so in God's strength.)

What role might a person with this gift have in the church today? (Though we all should seek to serve one another, people who are especially gifted in this area see what needs to be done and do it without being asked. They are usually the first to volunteer when someone expresses a need for help.)

3. Giving

There are several strong biblical examples of this gift. What does each of the following passages tell us about how to give?

Romans 12:8—(Give generously.)

II Corinthians 8:1-7—(Be eager to share, even beyond what you can reasonably afford.)

II Corinthians 9:1-8—(Give enthusiastically and cheerfully, not grudgingly, reluctantly, or out of compulsion.)

Mark 12:41-44—(Give sacrificially and faithfully.)

Acts 11:27-30—(Look for opportunities to give in times of special need.)

From this study, how would you define the gift of giving? (Giving willingly and generously to God's work and to the support of needy people.)

What role might a person with this gift have in the church today? (Though we all should give sacrificially, those who are especially gifted find a special joy in supporting God's work. In some cases, God has blessed them materially and given them a heart for giving back to Him.)

4. Leadership

How does Romans 12:8 say leaders are to lead? (Diligently.)

What else can we learn about leadership from Hebrews 13:7, 17? (It implies that leaders should live exemplary lives and are accountable for those they lead.)

We see a great example of leadership from Peter in Acts 15:5-11. What did he do there? (Peter recognized the problem, cut to the heart of the issue, reminded the people of God's Word, and proposed a course of action. That's leadership.)

Why is leadership considered to be a "serving" gift? (Mark 10:42-45) (In Christianity, leadership is service. Leaders must not lord it over anyone.)

From this study, how would you define the spiritual gift of leadership? (The ability to set a course of action and motivate people to follow.)

What role might a person with this gift have in the church today? (Pastor, teacher, program coordinator, committee chairman, board member, etc.)

5. Mercy

According to Romans 12:8, how should the gift of mercy be exercised? (Cheerfully.)

One good example of mercy is from Jesus' story of the good Samaritan (Luke 10:33-35). What did he do to show mercy to someone in need? (The good Samaritan took care of the wounded man's immediate needs, made arrangements for further care and lodging, then checked back to see how he was doing.)

What do Mark 9:41 and Matthew 25:34-40 teach us about showing mercy? (Merciful acts are rewarded [Mark 9:41]; it's really Christ to whom we are showing mercy [Matt. 25:34-40].)

Mercy seems to involve a feeling of compassion for someone in need. But what do James 2:15 and 16 say about expressing merciful feelings? (Feelings and words of mercy aren't enough. They must be backed by action.)

From this study, how would you define the spiritual gift of showing mercy? (The desire to care for suffering people and the ability to give the help they need.)

What role might a person with this gift have in the church today? (Though we all should show mercy, some people have a special awareness of needs around them and jump right in to give the needed help. These people might start or serve in a food-pantry ministry, or work with the benevolent fund.)

6. Faith

What does Mark 11:22-24 say about the potential power of faith? (Faith can move mountains; ask and receive.)

What can we learn from the following examples of biblical faith?

Acts 11:22-24—(Our faith can strengthen others and even result in conversions.)

Acts 27:21-25—(We can have confidence and peace and pass it on to others who are facing difficulties.)

Romans 4:18-21—(We can trust God to do what is humanly impossible.)

Putting all of that together, how would you define the spiritual gift of faith? (The ability to trust God and His promises even in difficult situations.)

What role might a person with this gift have in the church today? (Though we all need to trust God, some people just seem to trust Him more—and consistently. Able to encourage and inspire others when they begin to lose heart, these people might naturally be found in prayer or counseling ministries.)

7. Discernment

What guidance does I John 4:1-6 offer for "testing" spirits? (False spirits won't acknowledge Jesus in the correct, doctrinal way; they speak from the world's point of view, not God's; they are not as great as God, so we need not fear them.)

Biblical examples of discernment are found in Matthew 16:21-23 and Acts 5:1-11. Who discerned what? (Jesus discerned that Peter's advice was of Satan [Matt. 16:21-23]. Peter, ironically, later discerned that Ananias and Sapphira were lying about their gifts to the church [Acts 5:1-11].)

From this study and I Corinthians 6:5 and 6, what role might a person with this gift have in the church today? (We all need to develop a certain degree of discernment—to be aware of false teaching when it appears. But those who are gifted in this area are excellent judges of character. They work well on staff or lay committees that select personnel or curriculum. In an area only possibly related, I Corinthians 6:5, 6 indicates that believers can judge disputes among themselves without going to secular courts. A kind of discernment is necessary there, too.)

8. Administration

Jesus told a story of administration in Luke 14:28-30. What can we learn from it? (Before plunging into something, count the cost and evaluate the resources available—planning is crucial.)

Another biblical example is in Exodus 18:13-26. What can we learn from this? (Don't try to do everything alone; use all of the human resources available—delegate.)

The apostles were good administrators in Acts 6:1, 2. What was their problem and how did they solve it? (The apostles solved a food-distribution problem by delegating their authority to a group of deacons.)

From this study, how would you define the biblical gift of administration? (The ability to organize people to perform necessary tasks efficiently.)

What role might a person with this gift have in the church today? (People with the gift of administration make good Sunday school superintendents, heads of various age-level and special ministries, etc.)

5
Gifts at Work
(10-15 minutes)

Exploring the Use of Gifts
in a Church Situation

We've now examined sixteen gifts of the church. Now it's time to see how they work together. Explain to the group that they'll be doing an improvisation that will help to show how some of these different gifts interact. Ask for eight volunteers to "take" the following gifts:

> Discernment
> Administration
> Helping
> Mercy
> Hospitality
> Faith
> Encouragement
> Giving

Each gift-taker should have a good idea of what that gift is and how a person might use it. Appoint a ninth person as "the man" in the first improvisation (or play that part yourself).

Read the following situation to the group; then let them act it out. [Note: If your group is small, or time is limited, simply read the situation and brainstorm how people with each gift might help out.]

Situation 1—You are having a meeting at the church, when a shabbily dressed man comes to the door. He explains that he heard you were meeting and thought he might be able to get some help. He's been out of work for a while and has just been evicted from his apartment for not paying rent. His wife and baby son have gone to stay with a friend for a few days, but there's no room for him. He's not sure what to do.

Using your various gifts, how do you handle the situation? Act it out. (The *administrator* might organize and delegate responsibilities to those with the other gifts; the *discerning* person might determine the truth of the man's story and help him develop a plan of action; the *hospitable* person might invite the man to stay in his or her home for a few days; the *helper* might help the man find a job and an affordable place to live as soon as possible; the *giving* person might give the man money for immediate needs; the *merciful* person might provide the man with better clothes for job interviews; and the *encourager* might help the man realize the potential he has for the future; the person with the gift of *faith* might pray with conviction that God will act to supply this family's needs.)

When the scene has been played out, stop and talk about it:

How was each gift used?

Was there harmony among the various gifts, or was there some conflict?

Were there times when different gifts fit together to create something that neither gift could have created itself?

Were these gifts used for the good of the church and the glory of God? How?

If that goes well, and if there's time, you may want to try a second situation. See if anyone else wants to act, or if your actors want to try different gifts. Then choose one of the following:

Situation 2—Same meeting. The chairman reports that the

church needs a new building. The church's growth and the deterioration of the present facility require a new meeting place, which will demand a fund drive of major proportions. That might divert funds from other church ministries. Discuss the issue with your spiritual gifts in mind. [Note: You may want to add the gifts of *leadership* and *discernment*.]

Situation 3—Same meeting. Two active church members are running for the local school board—against each other. The campaign has turned nasty—with lies, gossip, and dirty tricks. The question has come up: Should the church do anything about this?

Situation 4—Same meeting. A church member has felt "called by God" to go to Ghana as a missionary. This person has made contact with a mission society and been approved, but the mission states that the home church must provide half of the missionary's support, a figure totaling $20,000 a year. Can the church commit itself to that expense? Discuss it with your gifts in mind. [Note: You or someone else may need to play the missionary.]

After each situation you do, debrief the group, using the same questions used in debriefing Situation 1.

6 Take Another

(5 minutes)

Allowing for Special Interest in Certain Gifts

Might any of these gifts belong to you? As we have talked about them, did any jump out at you or really interest you? You asked the same thing last time about the speaking gifts. Now see how the serving gifts appeal to people.

Once again, ask group members to take time this week to review Resource sheets 10 and 11 and consider whether they have any of these serving gifts.

Close in prayer, asking God for help in determining what gifts you have and how to use them.

If you'd like to prepare people for the next session, hand out copies of Resource 12, "Looking for Signs," for them to consider during the week.

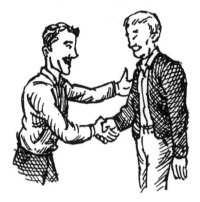

1. Hospitality

Note: The Greek word means "friendly to strangers."

People traveled a lot in the first century, and Christians often tried to stay with other Christians on their journeys. Note that Paul greeted many Romans by name (Romans 16), even though he'd never met them.

From examples in Romans 16:5, 23 and Acts 16:14, 15, what forms does hospitality in action take?

How does I Peter 4:9 say hospitality is to be extended?

Hospitality is a requirement for church leaders (I Timothy 3:2; Titus 1:8). Why would it be so important for these people?

From the Scriptures you've read so far, plus Hebrews 13:1-3 and Romans 12:13, how would you define the spiritual gift of hospitality?

What role might a person with this special gift have in the church today?

2. Helping (Service)

Note: Two Greek words are used. In I Corinthians 12:28, the word indicates "support, assistance," while in Romans 12:7 it indicates the service that a household slave would perform.

The Bible contains several strong examples of helping (Romans 16:1, 2; Acts 9:36-40; Luke 8:1-3; Mark 15:40, 41). What did these people do to help?

From your study so far, and I Peter 4:10 and 11, how would you define the biblical gift of serving/helping?

What role might a person with this special gift have in the church today?

SERVING GIFTS—I (CONT.)

3. Giving

There are several strong biblical examples of this gift. What does each of the following passages tell us about how to give?

Romans 12:8 _____

II Corinthians 8:1-7 _____

II Corinthians 9:1-8 _____

Mark 12:41-44 _____

Acts 11:27-30 _____

From this study, how would you define the gift of giving?

What role might a person with this special gift have in the church today?

4. Leadership

Note: The Greek word means simply "standing in front."

How does Romans 12:8 say leaders are to lead?

What else can we learn about leadership from Hebrews 13:7, 17?

We see a great example of leadership from Peter in Acts 15:5-11. What did he do there?

Why is leadership considered to be a "serving" gift? (Mark 10:42-45 gives a clue.)

From this study, how would you define the spiritual gift of leadership?

What role might a person with this special gift have in the church today?

5. Mercy

According to Romans 12:8, how should the gift of mercy be exercised?

One good example of mercy is from Jesus' story of the good Samaritan (Luke 10:33-35). What did he do to show mercy to someone in need?

What do Mark 9:41 and Matthew 25:34-40 teach us about showing mercy?

Mercy seems to involve a feeling of compassion for someone in need. But what does James 2:15, 16 say about expressing merciful feelings?

From this study, how would you define the spiritual gift of showing mercy?

What role might a person with this special gift have in the church today?

6. Faith

We all need faith for salvation, right? But the Bible also speaks of a powerful faith that characterizes certain people.

What does Mark 11:22-24 say about the potential power of faith?

What can we learn from the following examples of biblical faith?

Acts 11:22-24 _____

Acts 27:21-25 _____

Romans 4:18-21 _____

Putting all of that together, how would you define the spiritual gift of faith?

What role might a person with this special gift have in the church today?

Serving Gifts—II (cont.)

7. Discernment

In I Corinthians 12:10, this gift is called "distinguishing between spirits." What's that about? We don't think much about spirits these days, but the first-century church was well aware of the spiritual warfare going on around them. It was crucial for them to know when a particular teacher or leader or church member was motivated by the Holy Spirit, and when by an evil spirit (see Acts 20:30, 31; II Corinthians 11:12-15; Galatians 1:7).

What guidance does I John 4:1-6 offer for "testing" spirits?

Biblical examples of discernment are found in Matthew 16:21-23 and Acts 5:1-11. Who discerned what?

From this study and I Corinthians 6:5 and 6, what role might a person with this gift have in the church today?

8. Administration

Note: The Greek word is "governing," sometimes used for the steering of a ship.

Jesus told a story of administration in Luke 14:28-30. What can we learn from it?

Another biblical example is in Exodus 18:13-26, where Jethro helped Moses in an administrative matter. What can we learn from this?

The apostles were good administrators in Acts 6:1, 2. What was their problem and how did they solve it?

From this study, how would you define the biblical gift of administration?

What role might a person with this special gift have in the church today?

LOOKING FOR SIGNS

RESOURCE
12

Since we'll be talking about the "sign gifts" next session, pay attention to the signs you see this week—billboards, store signs, advertisements. Which ones really grab your attention, and which ones communicate a message or an image?

A sign that grabbed my attention:

How did it do that?

A sign that communicated a message or image the sign maker wanted to get across:

What was that message or image?

How did the sign communicate it?

DO I HAVE A SIGN GIFT?
Unraveling the Sign Gifts

Let's face it. It's hard to discuss the sign gifts—miracles, healing, tongues, interpretation of tongues—without offending someone. Many sincere, Bible-believing Christians take opposing views on the subject—some actively promote the sign gifts in the present day; others believe just as firmly that sign gifts ended with the early church. So the material in this session seeks to reveal what Scripture says and lets you, the group leader, draw the conclusions. [Note: As part of your preparation for this session, you may want to discuss this issue with your pastor.]

Whatever your conclusion on the subject, be prepared for those in your class who may disagree with your position. How will you handle any controversy that may arise? Use these guidelines:

(1) Stay with Scripture. Don't force an issue unless it's clearly biblical. (2) Avoid useless controversies. Don't drag the whole group into a fruitless argument (II Tim. 2:23, 24). (3) Remember that all spiritual gifts are for building up the church and for God's glory (I Cor. 14:4, 5). (4) "The greatest of these is love" (I Cor. 13:13).

Where You're Headed:
To help group members understand the four scriptural "sign" gifts and to consider their place in the church today.

Scriptures You'll Apply:
Acts 1—11, selected passages; I Corinthians 14

Things You'll Need:
- Bibles
- Copies of Resource 13, "Signs for These Times?"
- Copies of Resource 14, "Personal Gifts"
- Copies of Resource 15, "Your Opinion Counts"
- Pens or pencils and paper
- Chalkboard and chalk or newsprint and marker
- Three index cards (handwritten assignments for Step 1)

1
Marketing
Plan
(10-12 minutes)

Exploring the
Strategy of Signs

Divide into three groups. Give them all the following situation. **You own a store at [*the name of a shopping center near you*] Mall. Your store sells a cure-all that really works to make people healthier. Your group needs to design a front-window display to advertise your store and your product. Note also that there's an open area in front of your store where you could stage special events. You will be given slightly different strategies, but be creative. Plan your marketing approach, and go wild.**

Before sending the groups into three separate corners of the room, give writing materials and one of the following assignments (handwritten on an index card) to a volunteer group leader/reporter:

Group 1—**Your strategy is to attract attention. A lot of people walk by the store and don't even know it's there. Your presentation should let them know you're there.**

Group 2—**Your strategy is to prove that your cure-all really works. You've got this great product but some people think it's phony. Your presentation should convince people that it's for real.**

Group 3—**Your strategy is to show that respectable people do shop in your store and buy your product. A lot of people pass by your store thinking it would be foolish to enter. Your presentation should show how respectable your store is.**

Give groups five to eight minutes to plan their promotion, then call for group reports. Talk about the differences among the three groups. How did their plans differ? How did these plans reflect their differing goals? Note that there might be a progression from one goal to the next. A store might want to attract attention first, then prove its product, then enhance its image.

The early church had a similar situation. They had Christ's power within them, and they were taking His Gospel to a cynical world. God gave them certain "sign" gifts—miracles, healing, tongues, interpretation of tongues—not only to attract attention, but to validate what they were doing. But how effective were those gifts? And did their purposes change over time? Let's find out.

2
Whirlwind
Tour
(15-18 minutes)

Studying the Early
History of Sign Gifts

To see how these sign gifts functioned in the early church, we're going to take a "whirlwind tour" of the Book of Acts. Have the group turn in their Bibles to Acts 2. Then conduct the following question/answer session. Call on someone to read each passage before you ask the question:

Acts 2:1-4—**In a sentence, what happened here?** (The Holy Spirit came upon the disciples in a miraculous way. They began to speak in other tongues.)

Acts 2:5-8—**What was the effect of this miracle?** (People were amazed to hear the disciples speaking in their own languages.)

Acts 2:11-17—**According to verse 11, what was the content of the disciples' message?** ("The wonders of God.") **How did people react?** (Some wondered what it all meant; others mocked.) **What** did Peter say it meant? (It was the outpouring of the Spirit prophesied in Scripture.)

Acts 2:22—**What was the main point Peter wanted them to "listen" to?** (That Jesus was from God; later Peter spoke of Jesus' death and resurrection.) **How was Jesus "accredited by God"?** (By miracles, signs, and wonders. That is, God proved that He was empowering Jesus' ministry in this way.)

Review the following points, and write them on the chalkboard under the heading "MIRACLES—TONGUES":

• **This was a miraculous act of God that got people's attention.** Write "ACT OF GOD" and "TO GET ATTENTION."

• **The tongues-speaking was heard as real human language, not some angelic language.** Write "HUMAN LANGUAGE."

• **The tongues-speaking had content—"the wonders of God."** Write "SOLID CONTENT."

• **It seemed weird to some, even laughable.** Write "SEEMED WEIRD."

• **It demonstrated God's power.** Write "DEMONSTRATED GOD'S POWER."

• **It was used to testify about Jesus.** Write "TESTIFIED ABOUT JESUS."

Have group members look at Acts 2:42, 43. **Note that miracles were a part of the early church's life, and there was a sense of awe.** Beside the first heading, "MIRACLES—TONGUES," write "MANY MIRACLES." Under this second heading, write "PRODUCED AWE."

Now let's move on to Acts 3. Here, Peter and John encountered a lame man. Let's see what happened.

Acts 3:6-10—**What was the effect of this miracle?** (Wonder and amazement.)

Acts 3:12, 13—**What did Peter do with this "wonder and amazement"?** (He credited the miracle to God and testified about Jesus.)

Now let's skip to Acts 4. Here, Peter and John have been hauled before the authorities and interrogated about healing the lame man.

Acts: 4:13, 14—**What was the effect of the lame man's healing?** (It confounded the authorities. Essentially, it proved that Peter and John were working with God's power.)

Refer to the chalkboard. **We find some similar themes. This miracle gained attention and was turned to testify about Christ. It was convincing proof that the apostles' message was true.**

Acts 6:8—**Now *Stephen* is the miracle performer. Was he one of the apostles?** (No. He was a newly appointed deacon [6:3-5].)

Turn to Acts 8. Here, another deacon, Philip, was preaching in Samaria, where he encountered a sorcerer named Simon— someone who was used to doing miracles.

Acts 8:13—**What effect did Philip's miracles have on Simon?** (They won him over. He believed.) Explain that Peter and John arrived later and apparently presided over a meeting at which the Samaritan believers received the Holy Spirit. It doesn't say so, but this may have been accompanied by tongues-speaking. Whatever "signs and miracles" Simon saw, he was impressed by them.

Acts 8:18-20—**What did Simon want?** (He wanted to buy the ability to use the Holy Spirit. Old ways die hard. Simon saw this as a marketable gift. Peter and John quickly put a stop to that idea.)

Remember, this was a world in which spiritual power was evident. A sorcerer like Simon could work miracles through some demonic power. Since God's power went beyond his own power, Simon wanted it. Even after his conversion, Simon assumed that God's power was for sale. Write "SUPERIOR TO MIRACLES BY OTHER SPIRITS" under "PRODUCED AWE" on the board. **God's miracles regularly outdid those of demonic powers.**

Now turn to Acts 10:44-48. Here, Peter was sent by God to a Roman centurion who had believed in Christ. This centurion was among the first Gentiles (non-Jews) to be converted.

Acts 10:44-48—**How did the Jews in that group know that the Gentiles had received the Holy Spirit?** (The Gentiles spoke in tongues.) Write "ONE EVIDENCE OF CONVERSION" in the first column.

Your completed chalkboard summary should look like this:

MIRACLES—TONGUES
- ACT OF GOD
- TO GET ATTENTION
- HUMAN LANGUAGE
- SOLID CONTENT
- SEEMED WEIRD
- DEMONSTRATED GOD'S POWER
- TESTIFIED ABOUT JESUS
- ONE EVIDENCE OF CONVERSION

MANY MIRACLES
- PRODUCED AWE
- SUPERIOR TO MIRACLES BY OTHER SPIRITS

Skip to Acts 11. In this chapter, we discover that the Jewish believers back in Jerusalem weren't sure if non-Jews could be Christians too. But this is the argument Peter uses.

Acts 11:15-18—**How did the Jewish believers know that God had accepted the Gentiles?** (The Gentiles had received the Holy Spirit—which they knew through tongues-speaking.)

Acts 14:3—**Paul and Barnabas spoke boldly, doing signs and wonders. What was the purpose of those miracles?** (To confirm the message being preached.)

Acts 17:19, 20—**What miracles did Paul perform here?** Yes, this is the right passage! The answer is NONE! Note that Athens was a place where logic and reasoning were prized. They cared more about ideas than miracles. Therefore, we don't read of any miracles being performed there. This may be important for us as we try to understand why "signs and wonders" do not seem to be prevalent among Christians in the western world today. Perhaps some societies would not respond as well to the miracles. More about this later.

Review what you've written on the board. **What, in general, was the purpose of the sign gifts?** (To attract attention; to prove the truth of the Gospel and God's power; to convince Jewish Christians to welcome new groups of believers.)

3
Corinthian Cautions
(10-12 minutes)

Considering Some Biblical Second Thoughts

Something changed. From the time that Cornelius and the first Gentiles spoke in tongues to the time that Paul wrote his first letter to the Corinthians, something changed in this gift of tongues-speaking.

Ask someone to read I Corinthians 14:6-12. **What is the difference here about tongues-speaking from what we read in Acts?** ([1] Tongues-speaking has lost its content. [2] Tongues-speaking has become a "foreign" sound, not like the hometown languages of Acts 2. [3] In Corinth, tongues-speaking seems to be divisive, while in Acts it brought Christians together.)

Because of this difference, Paul urged several cautions. Quickly assign the following seven passages from I Corinthians to individuals or subgroups; then go through the passages, asking what cautions were recommended. [Note: You may want to summarize these cautions on the chalkboard as well.]

Cautions on tongues—I Corinthians:

13:1—(Without love, it's useless.)

14:1-3—(For public use, prophesying is better than tongues, because it edifies the church.)

14:12, 13—(Gifts are given to edify the church; unless there is an interpretation of what is said in tongues, speaking in tongues does not fulfill its purpose as a gift.)

14:18, 19—(Apparently, speaking in tongues is better in private.)

14:26—(Tongues is one of several gifts that can be used for strengthening the church.)

14:27, 28—(In church services, allow only two or three people to speak in tongues, one at a time, and then only if someone can interpret what they have said.)

14:32, 33—(Always maintain control, order, peace.) This is interesting—Paul said that, unlike the mystical ecstasies of other religions, tongues can and should be controlled by the speaker.

14:39, 40—(Prophesying is better, but don't forbid tongues—just allow it in a fitting and an orderly manner.)

Is this possible? Is it really possible to follow all of Paul's guidelines, or was he really just trying to discourage tongues-speaking and move the church on to more mature expressions? Opinions may vary. We'll sample a few in the next part.

4
Five Views
(8-10 minutes)

Hearing from Different Christian Voices

Hand out Resource 13, "Signs for These Times?" Different groups of Christians view the sign gifts in different ways, and this sheet expresses some of those views. Let's check them out. Your group members may agree with some and violently disagree with others.

With each view on the sheet, have someone read it, and then briefly discuss the position in light of the Scriptures just studied. [Note: If you have time and space, you may wish to set this up as a mock debate. Ask the five people who will be reading the different views to come up front and sit at a table facing the "audience." You might even make and place a sign in front of each debater, indicating which view he or she represents.]

Encourage honest reactions to each view, but don't get into a heated debate. Remember that the whole point of spiritual gifts is the building up of the body of Christ.

If your church takes an official stand on this issue, you may want to present it at this time. Otherwise, you may want to come to some consensus on which view best represents your group. If big differences exist, the most important thing to consider is this: How can we allow love, the most important quality of all, to help us live together in harmony on this issue as we strive to edify and build up one another and the church?

5
Homework
(5-8 minutes)

Beginning to Identify
Our Personal Gifts

It's exciting to realize that each one of us who is a Christian has been given a spiritual gift—something we can use for building up the church and glorifying God; something that, when discovered and used, will add a joy and fulfillment to our lives that we have never experienced before. Perhaps you already know or have a good idea what your gift is; or perhaps you still don't have a clue. Well, during our next session we'll concentrate on *finding* **our spiritual gifts. Some of you who already think you** *know* **what it is may be in for a surprise.**

At this point, I hope you feel the same anticipation you used to feel as a child when you went to bed on Christmas Eve. You are about to unwrap your *own* **spiritual gift! In preparation, there are two sheets you need to take home and bring back next time.** Hand out Resources 14 and 15, "Personal Gifts" and "Your Opinion Counts." **Fill out Resource 14 yourself. Take time to pray through it—to seek the Lord's direction. After you have written your name in the blank provided, give Resource 15 to a friend, spouse, or relative to get an outside opinion about what your spiritual gift might be. Have that person fill it out and give it back to you; then bring both resource sheets with you to our next session.** You may want to have extra copies of Resource 15 available in case some group members want to survey several outside sources.

[Note: If someone asks, these sheets are limited to the sixteen *speaking* and *serving* gifts—just because of the controversial nature of the *sign* gifts. If some people feel strongly that they have a sign gift, they should write that in on their sheet.]

Close in prayer, thanking God for the session and the spirit of peace that (it is hoped) was present. Pray for wisdom in taking this next step.

SIGNS FOR THESE TIMES?

1. NOW MORE THAN EVER

Miracles, healing, and tongues-speaking are needed now more than ever. God longs to work mightily through His church—but too many of us deny His power. Look around the world. He is confirming the Gospel by powerful signs in many lands, just as He did in New Testament days. These are gifts that we should cultivate in our churches. It's a simple matter of recognizing the gifts God is giving and being obedient in using them. Why are we so afraid of His power at work in us?

2. THAT WAS THEN, THIS IS NOW

The sign gifts were necessary in the early centuries of the church. God used these signs to communicate with His people. But now we have the Bible—that is how God communicates with us today. We no longer need messages in tongues. Paul himself spoke of the limited nature of tongues-speaking in I Corinthians. The church has moved beyond those spectacular gifts. Those who promote such gifts today are merely trying to manufacture certain experiences, and they run the risk of falling prey to fakery or even demonic influence.

3. PRIVATE MOMENTS

God may use tongues-speaking in His private interaction with certain believers. Perhaps they are so full of praise and love for Him that normal words will not suffice. God may grant them a heavenly language to use in communing with Him. If so, this is a private thing, and not to be foisted upon others. In I Corinthians 14, Paul himself spoke in tongues, but he seemed to discourage tongues-speaking in public. Perhaps miracles and healings work this same way. The confusion that would go along with any public expression of these gifts would just defeat the whole purpose.

—over—

Signs for These Times? (cont.)

4. New Ways for New Days

When a preacher like Billy Graham speaks and millions of people can hear him via a televised signal bounced off a couple of satellites, isn't that a miracle? When a doctor gives a patient a new heart, isn't that a healing? When Bible translators produce a New Testament in the language of some distant tribe, isn't that a gift of tongues or interpretation of tongues?

The world has changed in nineteen centuries. God has granted advances in technology and knowledge that the apostle Paul would have never dreamed possible. Modern "miracles" seem ordinary to us. We're used to them. But God grants them just the same.

5. When Necessary

The sign gifts should be handled with care. As in first-century Corinth, they are subject to abuse today. They are easily misunderstood, and they can quickly become the center of attention rather than a sign pointing to Christ. Especially in our cynical society, miracles, healings, and tongues-speaking would be generally ineffective as signs confirming the Gospel's truth.

But God works in mysterious ways. He may empower a Christian to lay hands on a sick friend and heal that person. Or in the right moment, for the right reason, He might enable a believer to work a miracle. Who are we to tell God He can't? But if we actively seek these sign gifts, reveling in their "spectacular" qualities, we confuse the sign with the reality and make an idol of it.

Spiritual gifts are Holy Spirit-empowered abilities that God has given to you for service and ministry in and through the church. (Remember, they are not job or career responsibilities or necessarily natural talents or skills.) In each of the four columns below, rank your top three gifts by numbering them 1, 2, and 3. (Note: The gift by which you put each of these numbers may vary in each column.)

Column W—*Want or desire*. Which three gifts would you most like to have?

Column R—*Related experience*. In which three areas have you found yourself involved in the church—whether you feel you have that gift or not?

Column A—*Ability*. In which three areas do you most excel?

Column P—*Prayer*. Leave this blank for a while, but pray about it during the week. Then if you feel God is guiding you in certain areas, rank His leading as well.

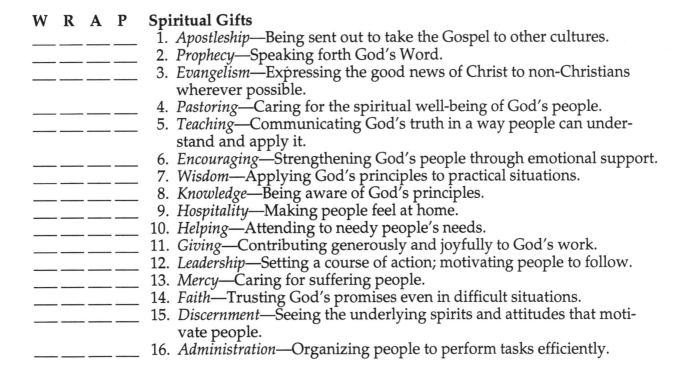

W R A P   Spiritual Gifts
_ _ _ _   1. *Apostleship*—Being sent out to take the Gospel to other cultures.
_ _ _ _   2. *Prophecy*—Speaking forth God's Word.
_ _ _ _   3. *Evangelism*—Expressing the good news of Christ to non-Christians wherever possible.
_ _ _ _   4. *Pastoring*—Caring for the spiritual well-being of God's people.
_ _ _ _   5. *Teaching*—Communicating God's truth in a way people can understand and apply it.
_ _ _ _   6. *Encouraging*—Strengthening God's people through emotional support.
_ _ _ _   7. *Wisdom*—Applying God's principles to practical situations.
_ _ _ _   8. *Knowledge*—Being aware of God's principles.
_ _ _ _   9. *Hospitality*—Making people feel at home.
_ _ _ _   10. *Helping*—Attending to needy people's needs.
_ _ _ _   11. *Giving*—Contributing generously and joyfully to God's work.
_ _ _ _   12. *Leadership*—Setting a course of action; motivating people to follow.
_ _ _ _   13. *Mercy*—Caring for suffering people.
_ _ _ _   14. *Faith*—Trusting God's promises even in difficult situations.
_ _ _ _   15. *Discernment*—Seeing the underlying spirits and attitudes that motivate people.
_ _ _ _   16. *Administration*—Organizing people to perform tasks efficiently.

Dear _____ ,

    Please complete the following gift analysis to help me determine my spiritual gifts. (Spiritual gifts are Holy Spirit-empowered abilities that God has given me for service and ministry in and through the church. They are not job or career responsibilities or necessarily natural talents or skills.)

    Read each gift title and its brief definition. Then put a check mark in the appropriate column on the left, indicating whether you think I *definitely* (**D**) have the gift or *maybe* (**M**) have the gift. If you think I *don't* have that gift, put nothing.

D   M   Gift List

  ___ ___ 1. **Apostleship**—Being sent out to take the Gospel to other cultures.

  ___ ___ 2. **Prophecy**—Speaking forth God's Word.

  ___ ___ 3. **Evangelism**—Expressing the good news of Christ to non-Christians wherever possible.

  ___ ___ 4. **Pastoring**—Caring for the spiritual well-being of God's people.

  ___ ___ 5. **Teaching**—Communicating God's truth in a way people can understand and apply it.

  ___ ___ 6. **Encouraging**—Strengthening God's people through emotional support.

  ___ ___ 7. **Wisdom**—Applying God's principles to practical situations.

  ___ ___ 8. **Knowledge**—Being aware of God's principles.

  ___ ___ 9. **Hospitality**—Making people feel at home.

  ___ ___ 10. **Helping**—Attending to needy people's concerns.

  ___ ___ 11. **Giving**—Contributing generously and joyfully to God's work.

  ___ ___ 12. **Leadership**—Setting a course of action and motivating people to follow.

  ___ ___ 13. **Mercy**—Caring for suffering people.

  ___ ___ 14. **Faith**—Trusting God's promises even in difficult situations.

  ___ ___ 15. **Discernment**—Seeing the underlying spirits and attitudes that motivate people.

  ___ ___ 16. **Administration**—Organizing people to perform tasks efficiently.

    Please return this letter to me by _____ .
Thanks for your help. Your opinion really matters to me.

Sincerely,

WHAT DID I GET? ◆
Discovering Our Specific Spiritual Gifts

In my family, putting clever tags on Christmas gifts has become a tradition. Once I got a coffee grinder from my parents, but the tag said, "TO RANDY FROM JUAN VALDEZ." This year I'm giving my brother a gift certificate from The Bombay Company. I may say it's "FROM GANDHI." You get the idea.

One year I got mixed up. I put the clever name on the "TO" part of the tag. Mom's cookbook was "TO JULIA CHILD." My sister's earrings were "TO VAN GOGH." Christmas morning brought confusion as I tried to remember who got what.

Maybe that's how some people in your group feel today. They've learned about the spiritual gifts in detail. They have all sorts of clues about their use. But who gets what? Today's session will help them learn how to identify their own gifts. It should be a time of great self-discovery and joy.

Where You're Headed:
To help group members identify their own spiritual gift(s) and plan how to use them.

Scriptures You'll Apply:
I Timothy 4:14-16

Things You'll Need:
- Bibles
- Copies of Resource 16, "Giftline"
- Copies of Resource 17, "Gift Discovery Test" (optional)
- Copies of Resource 18, "Gift Discovery Response Sheet"
- Copies of Resource 19, "My Gift" (optional)
- Pens or pencils
- Actors for the sketch on Resource 16
- Phone and horn (or other noisemaker) for sketch on Resource 16

1
Gift Radio
(5-10 minutes)

A Light Look at Some
Gift-finding Extremes

Begin with the skit on Resource 16, "Giftline." It requires just one "onstage" character—a talk-show host. The other voices can be provided by group members from their seats, by a single actor doing different voices, or by a prerecorded tape that the talk-show host runs.

Do the sketch, then briefly discuss it. **Let's see what this silly little sketch taught us about how to—and how *not* to—discover our own spiritual gifts.**

Can other people help us discover what our spiritual gifts are? (Yes!) **Why is getting someone else's opinion helpful?** (Obviously, each of us has an inside view, but those who know us can provide valuable outside opinions. We may be blind to some areas. Or we may be too "humble" to admit we're gifted in certain areas.)

How would you have answered some of those callers? (Certainly, Joey Charisma was no fountain of sensitivity. He should at least have been kinder to some callers. Your group may have other ideas, too.)

Do you think it's important to know what your spiritual gift is? Or should you just do what comes naturally? Why? (Perhaps some people can serve the church in various ways without pinning down a particular gift. But for others, discovering their gift is a matter of Christian identity, and they need to make decisions about how they will serve in the church most effectively. Also, "gifted" service brings personal satisfaction and joy, lessening the risk of burnout and guilt—see introduction on page 6.)

2
Treasure Hunt
(25-30 minutes)

Testing Our Inclinations
for Certain Gifts

We began this course by asking two basic questions: Who am I? Where do I fit in? At the time, how did we answer those questions? (Each of us is a gifted child of God, and we all fit together as the body of Christ.)

Now, in our last two sessions, each of us will find more specific answers to those questions. Not just "a gifted child," but "a child of God with such-and-such a gift." Not just a "part of the church body," but "Here's how I'll use my gift within the Body."

Ask how many remembered to bring back Resources 14 and 15, handed out last week. **We'll be looking at those sheets a little later, but first we're all going to take a test. It's one of those personality tests that basically just tells you what you tell it, but the mix of statements to which we respond may help some of us zero in on specific gifts.**

Hand out Resource 18, "Gift Discovery Response Sheet." **This is a response sheet for 48 statements I'll be reading. These statements correspond to the 48 numbered blanks on your sheet. For each statement I read, write a number from 1 to 5 next to the corresponding number. If you feel the statement is almost never true in your life, write "1"; if you feel the statement is almost always true of you, write down "5." Of course, the middle ground is 2 to 4. For the scoring to work, you must respond to** *every* statement.

Read the 48 statements on Resource 17, "Gift Discovery Test," allowing some time for people to respond to each statement before moving on. Make sure they get the number of each statement as you read it. [Note: You may prefer to have group members work through this test at their own speeds. If so, hand out copies of Resource 17 with Resource 18.]

When group members have responded to all of the statements, give the following instructions, allowing time for them to complete each one before moving to the next:

1. Total each line, adding *across* **each row. Put your total in the blank provided. For example, add responses to statements 1, 17, and 33, and put the total in the first box under "TOTAL."**

2. Circle any totals which are 12 or higher, and put a star by the highest total(s).

3. Now, beginning with the total for 1, 17, and 33, letter the totals from A to P.

To help group members interpret their tests, give out copies of Resource 17, "Gift Discovery Test," and direct their attention to the "Gift List" at the bottom of the second side of the sheet.

4. To discover your possible gifts, circle the letters in the gift list that correspond with the letters beside the highest totals you circled on Resource 18.

Interpreting the test:

• A score of 12 or more indicates the person *likely* has this gift.

• A score of 9 to 11 indicates the person *possibly* has this gift.

• A score of 8 or lower means the person *probably doesn't* have the gift.

Of course, this test is very simple, and not authoritative at all. Some statements may have been misunderstood. So don't use this test to rule *out* **any area just because you scored low in it. On the other hand, if you scored very high in several areas, don't assume that you are** *spiritually* **gifted in all of those areas. Simply use this test as** *one* **factor in a more thorough process of discovering your spiritual gift or gifts.**

3
The
Evidence
(5 minutes)

Collecting the Various
Clues about Our Gifts

You now have several elements in your search for your spiritual gifts. All of them contain clues that can help you answer the question "What did I get?"

You should have two sheets from last week—get those out now. One, Resource 14, contains your own opinions about your interests, abilities, experience—as well as any special cues from God you've received lately. All of those areas are important. When God gives you a spiritual gift, He usually puts a *desire* in your heart to use that gift. He also may give you *opportunities* to use those gifts—that's where the "experience" comes in.

The test you just took (Resources 17 and 18) should have confirmed what you wrote on Resource 14 this past week. You may notice that some of the statements to which you responded had to do with your desires—"I like to do such and such"; others involved experience—"People often ask me to do such and such"; or ability—"I'm good at doing such and such." If all of your repsonses converge on certain gifts, then you've got something.

Your other take-home sheet, Resource 15, was an outside opinion. All of us have blind spots. We need others to confirm or challenge our self-appraisal. We're about to take that a step further.

4
Feedback
(10-15 minutes)

Getting Others to Offer
Their Perspectives

Divide the group into subgroups of three people each. Explain that each person in these subgroups should reveal personal discoveries about his or her own spiritual gifts. Sharing insights from Resources 14, 15, and 18, each person should identify certain gifts he or she may have. The rest of the group may then comment on whether or not they agree on that gift and why.

Go over a couple of rules:

1. If you feel uncomfortable talking about your gifts, you may "pass."

2. If you challenge a person's idea of what his or her gift is, do so with Christian love. Be gentle and affirming.

Give subgroups up to ten minutes to share. Let them know when the time is half gone so everyone in each group will have a chance to speak. At the end of the time, bring everyone back together. Discuss: **Were there any surprises? Why? How did getting other people's feedback help you?**

5
The Next
Step
(5 minutes)

Launching into a Week of
Discovery and Verification

Read I Timothy 4:14-16. Reaffirm that first phrase—"Do not neglect your gift." [Note: If there's a question on the "laying on of hands," that was probably Timothy's ordination for pastoral work.]

Conclude by asking group members to take time this week to "nail down" the gifts they have. That is, if they still have any question about what gift they have, they should pray about it and seek counsel.

Next time we'll take specific steps toward using our gifts. If you'd like to do some advance thinking about this, here's a sheet that can help you. Give a copy of Resource 19, "My Gift," to anyone who's interested.

Close in prayer, thanking God for His great gifts.

GIFTLINE

JOEY: Hey, everyone out there in Radioland, this is Joey Charisma doing the eight to twelve gig on Giftline, the show that's all about spiritual gifts. If you're out there wondering what you've got, where to get it, or what to do with it—this is the place to call: 555-7777. That's 555, all 7s. Hey, we've got a caller. Welcome to Giftline.

CALLER 1: Hi, Joey?

JOEY: Right here, guy, talking on Giftline.

CALLER 1: Am I on?

JOEY: Yes, you are. And a couple million people are listening with bated breath. Hey, do me a favor. Turn down your radio. That seven-second delay's a killer.

CALLER 1: Is that better?

JOEY: You're on, my friend. What's your question?

Caller 1: Well, I don't think I have a spiritual gift.

JOEY: What makes you think that?

CALLER 1: Well, I'm just not good at *anything*. Now my sister, she's really wise and friendly. She's always teaching me stuff. She probably has *every* gift in the Book. But not *me*. I don't have *anything*.

JOEY: Hmmm. That's a tough one. You say your sister has spiritual gifts?

CALLER 1: Yeah.

JOEY: And she uses them pretty well?

CALLER 1: Oh, yeah, she's great!

JOEY: And do you ever tell her so?

CALLER 1: Sure. All the time.

JOEY: Then that's ENCOURAGEMENT! We have a winner! *[Toots horn.]* Next caller, please. What's your gift?

CALLER 2: Well, I don't know where to start. I have so *many*.

JOEY: You do, huh? Well, how about teaching? You got that?

CALLER 2: Oh, sure. I'm a *great* teacher, and a *natural* leader, and a *phenomenal* administrator. I also have the gifts of wisdom, healing, serving, hospitality, and encouragement!

JOEY: I think you forgot one.

CALLER 2: What's that?

JOEY: HUMILITY! *[Hangs up.]* Hey there, you're on Giftline.

CALLER 3: I have a really strong feeling of rejection. Is that a spiritual gift?

JOEY: Nope. *[Hangs up.]* Next caller. You're on Giftline.

CALLER 4: There's this gift I have. I've been trying to use it, but everyone gets mad at me when I do.

JOEY: What's that?

CALLER 4: EVERYONE GETS MAD AT ME WHEN I DO! What, are you deaf?

JOEY: No, I mean, what gift are you trying to use?

CALLER 4: Well, it's right there in the Bible. I don't see why anyone would have a problem with it.

JOEY: Well, what is the gift?

CALLER 4: Hostility. *[Pause]* You gotta problem with that?

JOEY: It's hospitality, Bozo. Hospitality, not hostility.

CALLER 4: Oh, never mind.

JOEY: Hey there! You're on Giftline.

CALLER 5: Joey, I have the gift of discernment, and I think you are a phony. You know nothing about gifts or how to use them. You are a total fraud.

JOEY: Very nicely said. A powerful comment. As you have probably discerned, I have the gift of encouragement. Call again sometime. We need more callers like you. *[Hangs up.]* You're on Giftline.

CALLER 6: Joey, this is Lou. Your cousin.

JOEY: Hey, Lou, what's up?

CALLER 6: I think I have the gift of administration.

JOEY: Why's that, Lou?

CALLER 6: I like to sit around and tell everyone else what to do.

JOEY: No, Lou, I don't think so. That's a common mistake. But I'm afraid you have the gift of BEING A LAZY BUM. Catch ya later, Cuz. Next caller.

CALLER 7: Joey, I think I know what my gift is, but I haven't found any way to use it.

JOEY: I know. That can be a real problem.

CALLER 7: It's really frustrating when you want to be faithful, but you don't have an outlet. And I have so very much to give, I just don't know where. You know what I mean?

JOEY: I'd love to talk with you more about this, but we're just about out of time. So what did you say your gift was?

CALLER 7: Giving. You know, *contributing*— like money!

JOEY: Well, hey, we've got a few moments. Let's talk. I think I can help you. The name is Joey Charisma. With a C-H. And you can send that check right here to me at Giftline, 12-B Rich Avenue, that's 1—2—B Rich Avenue. Got that? Right here in Our Town. Any amount would be fine, but why not let me help you with the whole thing? I'm happy to be of service to you. SERVICE! *[Blows horn.]* There's another! The gifts are hoppin' here on Giftline, but that's all we have time for. I'm losing my voice here, and you know what they say: "Don't book a gift mouth when he's hoarse." Catch ya later, on GIFTLINE!

GIFT DISCOVERY TEST

Test Questions:

Respond to each of the following statements, using Resource 18, "Gift Discovery Response Sheet."

1. I am good at planning things.
2. I believe God is calling me to be a "missionary" in some area of great need.
3. I can spot a phony before anyone else can.
4. I see the potential in a person, even if that person is presently struggling.
5. I enjoy sharing my faith with others whenever the opportunity arises.
6. God answers my prayers very specifically.
7. I enjoy giving money to worthy causes.
8. When I see newcomers at church, I hurry to make them feel welcome.
9. I really enjoy studying the Bible and learning more and more.
10. People look to me to decide what a group will do.
11. I identify with people who are hurting.
12. I have a desire to care for new Christians' spiritual welfare.
13. In my Bible study, I see how society's ways need to change.
14. I see things that need to be done, and I do them.
15. I enjoy guiding others in discovering Bible truth and applying it to their lives.
16. I can see a solution to a difficult crisis, even if no one else can.
17. I find great joy in organizing projects and new ministries.
18. I like to *help* organize and start new ministries.
19. I can see through people's actions and know their inner motives.
20. People tell me about their problems, and I don't really mind.
21. I am concerned for people who don't know Christ.
22. I am more optimistic than others about what God will do in our church.
23. When I hear of a new ministry, I offer financial support even before anyone asks me.
24. I enjoy using my home or other resources to meet people's needs.
25. I have learned a great deal by listening to pastors and Bible teachers.
26. If in a situation that lacks organization, I step forward to provide leadership.
27. I strongly desire to help others—even if they can't return my favors.
28. I think about how others are doing spiritually, and I want to help in any way I can.
29. When people tell me their problems, I respond with a message from God's Word.
30. I like to pitch in and do the "dirty work" that helps others fulfill their ministries.
31. When I explain something, people seem to understand.
32. I like to see how biblical truth can help resolve thorny issues.
33. If I am in a situation that lacks organization, I try to get someone to take the lead.
34. I am good at envisioning something before it happens, and I know how to make it happen.
35. I am very critical of teachers who stray from the clear teaching of God's Word.
36. I feel very fulfilled when I say things that help other people deal with tough times.
37. When I talk about my faith, unbelievers seem to understand and be interested.
38. I encourage other Christians to trust God and think big.
39. I believe that everything I own belongs to God and I use everything I have for His glory.
40. If some church group is arranging a social event, they know they can count on me to host it.

41. People ask for my opinion on difficult Bible texts.
42. I like the challenge of assessing a group's needs and motivating the group to meet its goals.
43. In group meetings, I'm more concerned with people's feelings than with what they're saying.
44. When someone strays from the faith, I'm deeply troubled and want to help restore that person.
45. I feel that God is using me to express a specific message to someone else.
46. I am more of a "behind-the-scenes" person than an "up-front star."
47. I enjoy talking to groups and explaining things about the Bible.
48. People ask me for advice.

Further Instructions:

After you have written your responses on Resource 18, follow these instructions to zero in on your possible spiritual gifts:

1. Add up the three figures in each row, going *across*. Put each total in the blank provided.
2. Circle any totals which are 12 or higher and put a star by the highest total(s).
3. Letter the totals from A to P, beginning with the first total.
4. Then, circle the letters in the Gift List below that correspond with the letters by the totals you circled on Resource 18.

GIFT LIST
A. Administration
B. Apostleship
C. Discernment
D. Encouragement
E. Evangelism
F. Faith
G. Giving
H. Hospitality
I. Knowledge
J. Leadership
K. Mercy
L. Pastoring
M. Prophecy
N. Helping
O. Teaching
P. Wisdom

Interpreting the Test:

- A score of 12 or more indicates that you *probably* have this gift.
- A score of 9 to 11 indicates you *possibly* have this gift.
- A score of 8 or lower means you *probably don't* have the gift.

Caution: Don't use this test to rule *out* any gift; simply use it as one factor in a more thorough process of discovering your spiritual gift or gifts.

[Note: Some statements in this test have been adapted by permission from *How to Discover Your Spiritual Gifts,* by Clyde B. McDowell, © 1988, Lay Action Ministry Program, 5827 S. Rapp St., Littleton, Colo. 80120.]

GIFT DISCOVERY RESPONSE SHEET

The 48 numbers below correspond with the 48 statements on Resource 17. After each numbered statement is read (either by you, or aloud by your leader), indicate the degree to which each statement is true of you by putting a number from 1 to 5 in the corresponding space provided.

DEGREE
1 = Almost never
2 = Some of the time
3 = It depends
4 = A lot of the time
5 = Almost always

Statement/Responses			Totals
1.____	17.____	33.____	_____
2.____	18.____	34.____	_____
3.____	19.____	35.____	_____
4.____	20.____	36.____	_____
5.____	21.____	37.____	_____
6.____	22.____	38.____	_____
7.____	23.____	39.____	_____
8.____	24.____	40.____	_____
9.____	25.____	41.____	_____
10.____	26.____	42.____	_____
11.____	27.____	43.____	_____
12.____	28.____	44.____	_____
13.____	29.____	45.____	_____
14.____	30.____	46.____	_____
15.____	31.____	47.____	_____
16.____	32.____	48.____	_____

When you have responded to all of the statements,
refer to "Further Instructions" on the bottom of Resource 17.

MY GIFT

Discovering and using your spiritual gift(s) is somewhat like solving a puzzle. When all the pieces fit, you make an exciting discovery and have a sense of real fulfillment. So be thinking about your main spiritual gift this week—What is it? How can you use it? Look for others who seem to have your gift. What are they doing? What can you learn from them?

I think my gift might be:

_____

Some possible ways I could use this gift are:

Somebody I know who seems to have this gift:

_____

Something I could learn from this person:

HOW CAN I USE IT?
Learning to Use Our Spiritual Gifts

Once upon a time, a boy received a beautiful gift from an uncle who lived far away. It was a baseball bat, the best that money could buy, carefully carved from the finest wood. The only problem was, the boy didn't have a baseball, nor did anyone he knew. Furthermore, neither he nor his friends knew how to play, and there were no fields nearby. So, though the baseball bat was a lovely gift, he couldn't use it.

Sometimes gifted Christians may feel as that boy felt. They have great gifts from God but for some reason are unable to use them. Perhaps the church isn't "ready" for their type of ministry. Perhaps that ministry is filled with gifted people and has no available openings. Perhaps it's just that no one is helping those people find their place in the church.

All of our work in helping people understand and identify spiritual gifts does little good unless we can take the next step—putting people to work, using their gifts for the good of the church and God's glory.

Where You're Headed:
To inspire group members to use their spiritual gifts and to help them develop a plan for doing so.

Scriptures You'll Apply:
Romans 12:1-5

Things You'll Need:
- Bibles
- Copies of Resource 20, "Superguy Overboard"
- Copies of Resource 21, "Job Possibilities"
- Copies of Resource 22, "Action Plan"
- Pens or pencils and extra paper
- Chalkboard and chalk or newsprint and marker
- Preparation of actor(s) to do the skit on Resource 20
- Information on church ministries—whom to see or call to get involved.

1
Untapped Resources
(5-10 minutes)

A Light Look at the Tragedy
of Unused Gifts

You'll need three actors prepared to do the skit on Resource 20, "Superguy Overboard." (Only Clint Kark needs to be male.) Introduce the skit by saying, with dramatic flare: **And now, our not-ready-for-prime-time players present "Superguy Overboard"! The meek and mild Clint Kark, really Superguy in disguise, has just walked into a bank and is seated at—a loan officer's desk?**

After the skit is performed, talk about it. **In light of the gifts we have as Christians, what's the point of this skit?** (The point is very simple: How ridiculous it would be for Superguy to avoid using his powers. Yet in *real* life, we Christians have God-given power and often fail to use it. That's more ridiculous.)

Today, we'll discover ways to use our spiritual gifts and take steps to make it happen.

2
Living Sacrifices
(10-15 minutes)

General Principles for
Using Our Gifts

Have the group turn to Romans 12. **This chapter offers some general principles we can apply to using our spiritual gifts.** Be ready to write key thoughts on the chalkboard. Have someone read each verse before you ask the questions related to it.

Romans 12:1—**What does Paul urge us to do?** (Offer our bodies as living sacrifices.)

What is a "living sacrifice"? (In Old Testament times, sacrifices were often animals that were brought to God's altar and killed as symbols of payment for sin or signs of gratitude or commitment. A *living* sacrifice would be the commitment of one's whole life to God.)

How does Paul describe these sacrifices? (Holy and acceptable to God.)

How does that apply to us? (Just as the Old Testament sacrifices were to be animals of good quality—holy and acceptable—so we should lead holy lives that please God.)

What does Paul mean by "spiritual worship"? (The idea is that, in a spiritual way, we can do the same sort of service that the priests did in the temple. The word for worship here is the one for "acts of worship" performed by priests or Levites. This fits in nicely with the discussion of spiritual gifts. The priests and Levites would have their assigned tasks—their "acts of worship"—to perform. In a spiritual way, we believers have our assigned tasks—the gifts we've been given—and we need to throw our whole selves into them.) Write "OFFER WHOLE SELVES" on the chalkboard.

Romans 12:2—**In this verse there's something we shouldn't do, something we should do, and a result. What are each of these?** (*Don't* conform to this world. *Do* be transformed by allowing God to renew our minds. The *result* is that God's perfect desires are played out in us.)

What do you think the "renewing of our minds" has to do with spiritual gifts? Why would that be necessary? (Worldly ways of thinking might lead us to pride or selfishness in the use of our gifts. We need God's priorities.) Write on board "RENEWED

MINDS. "

Romans 12:3—**What attitudes should we have in using our gifts?** (Humility and realism. Obviously, we can't enter a situation saying, "I'd better use my gifts here, or else!" We need to find our realistic place in the Body.) Write on the board: "REALISTIC VIEW."

Have group members skim Romans 12:4-8. **We're back where we started: the giving of gifts.** Look back at the chalkboard and review the points:

• OFFER WHOLE SELVES—**We need to offer our whole selves, gifted as we are, to God's service.**

• RENEWED MINDS—**We need to let God change our ways of thinking.**

• REALISTIC VIEW—**We need to have a realistic view, and certainly not a proud view, of our own value to the church body.**

3
Possibilities
(10-15 minutes)

Considering the Options for
Using Our Gifts

Hand out Resource 21, "Job Possibilities." **With those principles in mind, let's start figuring out the specific tasks we could do with the gifts we have.** For each gift, Resource 21 lists several tasks that might be performed in a typical church. Your church may or may not be typical. So, for each gift, you should discuss whether there are other tasks in your church that would fit. Have group members write in the additional tasks, especially for the gifts they think they have.

As you go, you will find a great deal of overlap. For instance, Sunday school teachers might be gifted with one or more of the following gifts: teaching, prophecy, knowledge, wisdom, pastoring, leadership, or several other gifts.

You will also find that other interests and talents now begin to come into play. For instance, a talented soloist may have the gift of prophecy—and thus might use his or her gift and talent together, singing songs that challenge the congregation with God's truth. A sports buff might have the gift of encouragement—and would thus be perfect to coach the softball team. Remember: We are giving our whole selves to the Lord. God uses our natural talents, interests, training, and experience in conjunction with our spiritual gifts.

After you have gone through Resource 21, give the group a minute or two to look over the options. Ask them to think about the tasks where they could use their spiritual gifts. Have them write some of their ideas on the back of the sheet (or supply them with an extra piece of paper).

4
Action Plan
(20-25 minutes)

Getting Group Input on
Specific Steps

Now divide into groups of three to five people each and give everyone a copy of Resource 22, "Action Plan." (If you can duplicate the groups of last session, great.)

Assuming that we all now know what our gifts are, the question is, How will we use them?

Each of you, with the help of your small group, should come up with a written Action Plan. This plan will not only name a certain opportunity or ministry in which to get involved, but will also list whatever steps are necessary to make that happen. In many cases, it will be a phone call to the head of that ministry, volunteering your services. In some cases, it might involve training or apprenticeship. (Remember: Don't think of yourselves more highly than you ought.)

Each small group may offer advice or even connections. As the leader, you should be prepared with names (and phone numbers?) of the church's key ministry leaders. Circulate among the small groups and offer this assistance where necessary.

Some of your group members will already be as involved as they want to be. That's fine. Don't push them to add a new activity to an already packed schedule, but challenge them to evaluate whether their present activities match their gifts. Primarily, this step is for those who are trying to find their place, who want to find new areas of involvement within the church. Challenge those people to come up with at least one concrete step ("Call So-and-so") thatthey can accomplish in the next week.

When you have given time for this, ask volunteers to share their Action Plans with the whole group. Make a personal note to check up on these people a month from now, to see how they're doing. Invite any other testimonies people may have about how this course has affected their lives.

Encourage each small group to spend some time in prayer together, thanking God for the gifts He has given them and committing themselves to follow through on their Action Plans. [Note: To encourage accountability, you might suggest that group members leave copies of their Action Plans with you. In four or five weeks, mail the Action Plans back to the originators as reminders of the commitments they made today.]

SUPERGUY OVERBOARD

The scene begins with Clint Kark *(Superguy in disguise) seated in front of a desk. Loan officer* Mary, *seated behind the desk, is looking over his loan application.*

MARY: So, Mr. Kark, you want a loan. Is that right?

CLINT: Yes. It's just been a tough time for me lately. I'm way behind on my bills.

MARY: Yes, I've been hearing a lot of that. Now it says here that you have a part-time job as a reporter.

CLINT: Well, yes. They don't pay very well.

MARY: Any chance of making that full-time?

CLINT: I'm afraid not. The Universe has been in pretty bad shape.

MARY: You're telling me!

CLINT: No, I mean the newspaper. The Daily Universe. Where I work. Part-time.

MARY: Oh, of course. I knew that. Now it says here you have another part-time job. *[Reading]* Supper—?

CLINT: *[whispering]* Superguy.

MARY: What was that?

CLINT: *[a bit louder]* Superguy. You know, with the cape. Faster than a speeding bullet?

MARY: Oh, of course! You're *that* Clint Kark. I should have recognized you.

CLINT: That's okay. I really try to keep it a secret. People hear you've got superhuman powers and they want the world from you, you know? It's "fix this" and "save him" and "jump over that building." It can get tiring.

MARY: I can imagine. *[returning to papers]* So does this Superguy work pay very well?

CLINT: Not lately. Well, I haven't been working that much.

SUPERGUY OVERBOARD (CONT.)

MARY: Why not? I would think with all the crime on the streets—

CLINT: It's not my problem, okay?

ROBBER: *[bursting in]* All right! This is a stickup! Everybody put your hands up!

MARY: Superguy, do something. Here's your chance.

CLINT: What exactly do you want me to do?

MARY: Stop the bank robber! Save us all!

CLINT: But then everybody would know I'm Superguy and I'd have to sign autographs and all that.

ROBBER: *[to a cashier offstage]* Now just give me the money. No talking over there!

MARY: It's okay. He's Superguy.

ROBBER: Yeah, and I'm the Yellow Hornet.

CLINT: No, he's actually much shorter.

ROBBER: You trying to make trouble?

MARY: Yes, he is!

CLINT: No, I'm really very mild-mannered.

MARY: He could stop your bullets with his bare hands!

ROBBER: *[a sudden realization]* Bullets! I knew I forgot something. I'm out of here.

MARY: Get him, Superguy!

CLINT: Don't call me that.

MARY: He's getting away! Stop him!

CLINT: Let's talk loan first. Then I'll see if I can track him down.

MARY: If you insist. Now, do you have any collateral, Mr. Kark?

CLINT: Well, I have some stock in a chain of phone booths.

JOB POSSIBILITIES

A. Administration
Boards/committees
Project coordinator
Office management
Long-range planning
Sunday school superintendent
Financial secretary

B. Apostleship
Missions
Church planting
Inner-city, prison, campus,
hospital, youth ministry
Short-term mission project
Developing a new ministry

C. Discernment
Nominating committee
Youth ministry
Counseling
One-to-one discipleship
Hiring/staffing selection

D. Encouragement
Counseling
Sunday school teaching
Coaching
Ministry recruiting
Youth ministry
Writing articles for newsletter

E. Evangelism
Greeter
Missions
Investigative Bible studies
Visitation
Inner-city prison, campus,
hospital, youth ministry

F. Faith
Planning
One-to-one discipleship
Prayer chain
Fund-raising

G. Giving
Stewardship board
Ministries to the poor
Missions support
New project start-up

H. Hospitality
Home Bible study
Visitation
Singles Ministry
Greeter
Usher
Social event planning

JOB POSSIBILITIES (CONT.)

I. Knowledge
Sunday school teaching
Planning
Writing curriculum for
  special classes
Preaching
Library management
Small group leader
_____

J. Leadership
Chairperson of a committee
Song leader / Worship leader
Project manager
Coaching
_____

K. Mercy
Hospital visitation
Prayer chain
Administration of deacon's fund
Counseling
Food collection / distribution
_____

L. Pastoring
Pastor / Elder / Deacon
Lay leader
One-to-one discipleship
Absentee follow-up
Bible study leader
Youth leader
_____

M. Prophecy
Preaching
Singing solos
Writing
Bible study leader
_____

N. Serving
Nursery
Office help
Project coordinator
Technical support
Music / drama management
Computer consultation
Facility set-up
_____

O. Teaching
Sunday school teacher
Writing
Youth ministry
Bible study leader
One-to-one discipleship
Coaching
_____

P. Wisdom
Administrative board
Counseling
Nominating committee
Small group leader
_____

[Some of this material is adapted by permission from *How to Discover Your Spiritual Gifts,* by Clyde B. McDowell, © 1988 by Lay Action Ministry Program, Littleton, Colo. 80120.]

ACTION PLAN

Name: _____

GIFT(S)

_____

_____

_____

POSSIBLE OPPORTUNITIES

_____

_____

_____

CONTACT PERSON

_____

_____

_____

PHONE NUMBER

_____

_____

_____

STEPS TO USING MY GIFT(S)

1. _____

2. _____

3. _____

TARGET DATE

_____

_____

_____